When Gospels Collide

When Gospels Collide

Robert M. Price

AN IMPRINT OF THE
GLOBAL CENTER FOR RELIGIOUS RESEARCH
1312 17TH STREET • SUITE 549
DENVER, COLORADO 80202

INFO@GCRR.ORG • GCRR.ORG

GCRR Press
An imprint of the Global Center for Religious Research
1312 17th Street Suite 549
Denver, CO 80202
www.gcrr.org

DOI: 10.33929/GCRRPress.2021.04

Unless otherwise noted, Scripture quotations are from Revised Standard Version of the Bible, copyright © 1946, 1952, and 1971 National Council of the Churches of Christ in the United States of America. Used by permission. All rights reserved worldwide.

Copyeditor/Proofreader: Christian Farren
Cover Design: Darren M. Slade

Library of Congress Cataloging-in-Publication Data

When gospels collide / Robert M. Price
p. cm.
Includes bibliographic references (p.).
ISBN (Print): 978-1-7378469-8-7
ISBN (eBook): 978-1-7378469-9-4
1. Bible—Gospels—Criticism, interpretation, etc.   2. Hermeneutics—Religious aspects—Christianity.   3. Bible—Evidences, authority, etc.   4. Bible—Language, style.   I. Title.

BS2350-2393   .P753   2021

❧

I dedicate this book to my wonderful wife Qarol,
without whom I would doubtless be living in a sleeping bag under the
escalator at the Port Authority Bus Terminal.

A Selection of Book Publications By Robert M. Price

Beyond Born Again: Towards Evangelical Maturity (Hypatia Press, 1993)

Deconstructing Jesus (Prometheus Books, 1999)

The Incredible Shrinking Son of Man (Prometheus Books, 2004)

The Empty Tomb: Jesus beyond the Grave (Prometheus Books, 2005)

The Pre-Nicene New Testament (Signature Books, 2006)

Jesus Is Dead (American Atheist Press, 2007)

Blaming Jesus for Jehovah: Rethinking the Righteousness of Christianity (Tellectual Press, 2015)

The Amazing Colossal Apostle: The Search for the Historical Paul (Signature Books, 2012)

Jesus Christ Superstition (Pitchstone Publishing, 2019)

Judaizing Jesus: How New Testament Scholars Created the Ecumenical Golem (Pitchstone Publishing, 2021)

Advanced Endorsements

Dr. Robert Price is one of the most creative scholars in the field of Biblical Scholarship, and one of the most snubbed and misunderstood. One does not need to agree with his interpretations of ancient texts to appreciate the range of his interests and his imaginative evaluation of them and their relevance to the modern world. His should be a welcome alternative voice to the stodginess of contemporary biblical scholarship. I often have been amazed at the breadth of his reading in ancient literature and modern scholarship, his grasp of ancient mythology, and his courage to challenge the ignorant shiboleths of so many publications about the Bible. Dr. Price knows that we often disagree, but my engagement with his informed and thoughtful interpretations has enriched my scholarship. That no doubt will be the experience of many readers of this publication.

–Dennis R. MacDonald,
Emeritus Professor, Claremont School of Theology

With profound honesty and scholarly rigor, Price reveals how the contradiction and incoherence that suffuse the Christian Gospels conceal a treasury of insight for the mature reader. A powerful look at the creative diversity of earliest Christian traditions.

–Dr. Richard C. Miller,
Author of *Resurrection and Reception in Early Christianity*

The erudite and always entertaining Robert Price has produced another lively, informative book with a premise many may find challenging: that the contradictions between the gospels provide a veritable gold mine of valuable information about the uneven *early* evolution of *early* Christianity. A great read!

–Russell Gmirkin,
Author of *Berossus and Genesis, Manetho and Exodus*

Contents

Introduction

Why would readers of the Bible fear having to admit the presence of contradictions in their sacred text? And it *is* fear, as anyone can see from the lengths that fundamentalists will go to resolve them. Contradictions must be ironed out, "harmonized," because they believe biblical contradictions are like Kryptonite to Superman. The superpowers of the Superbook would be drained by contradictions. The supernatural book would collapse and die from exposure to the poison radiating from those contradictions. In other words, the Bible could no longer be esteemed as the Word of God. It could no longer dictate your life and your beliefs,—which is just what you want it to do. Why? Because people have been taught to imagine God as a peevish theology professor who will send you down the chute into hell if you get too many answers wrong on that postmortem final exam. And to prepare for that examination, you need a textbook to give you the infallible answers. You dare not rely on guess work! How would you know how many persons are in the Godhead if that information were not forthcoming from a divine source? And if one passage disagrees with another, how would you know which one to believe? *If either*? Because the mere presence in Scripture of a notion could not any longer guarantee its truth. And then you're up the creek!

The upshot is that this model just does not work. It does not fit the data, or what evangelical theologians call "the phenomena of Scripture." As Clark H. Pinnock, himself an evangelical theologian, once said, "The fundamentalists don't like the Bible they've got."[1] In Thomas Kuhn's classic book, *The Structure of Scientific Revolutions*, he relates how researchers start shopping

---

[1] Comment during a lecture at New College in Berkeley, CA in 1978.

around for a new interpretive paradigm when too many "anomalous data" has accumulated, data that just does not fit the old one.[2] And there *is* an alternative paradigm if one finds oneself compelled to abandon biblical inerrancy. It has been around for a couple of centuries and seems to work very well: the historical-critical method. The trouble is that it only works if you stop insisting that the Bible is a divinely inspired book, infallible and inerrant. But does that not mean it is useless as a magical answer book? Darn right. But maybe the unworkability of the fundamentalist approach should tip people off that it is the *wrong* approach. And that, in turn, the God-concept upon which that approach is predicated is equally wrong.

If the Bible has shown itself not to be infallible as history or a trustworthy textbook of otherwise unverifiable doctrines, how *do* we approach it? We recognize it as *literary* in character, a book that does indeed embody various beliefs and ethics but, by the use of various genres, contains many non-factual teachings in either intent or effect. Therefore, it is not infallible. *Wise* is not good enough?

And if we make this major shift, contradictions can be seen in an entirely new light. We will find there is nothing to be afraid of anymore. But more than that, contradictions turn out to be good, not bad. They do not mar the Bible but actually decorate it! On the fundamentalist model, contradictions would have to be written off as stupid goofs made by stupid writers. Indeed, disillusioned ex-fundamentalists still look at it that way. They still hold to the literalist model except that they now view the Bible as no longer prophecy but as *false* prophecy. They are just as wrong as the theological apologists. The "contradictions" are mostly *redactions*, edits, updates, and reasoned modifications aimed at making new points. Such differences are keys to a far greater and deeper understanding of the Bible. Some may find that prospect disappointing: the Bible is no longer seen to be the supernatural answer book they wanted it to be and thought they needed it to be.

---

[2] Thomas S. Kuhn, *The Structure of Scientific Revolutions* (Chicago: University of Chicago Press, 1962), "Anomaly and the Emergence of Scientific Discoveries," pp. 52–61.

But if you love the Bible for its own sake, as I do, you will have lost nothing and gained much.

In the present book, I will consider, one by one, pairs or sets of contradictions between Gospels, sometimes within a single Gospel. I will venture to explain the differences by indicating what the writer or redactor was driving at. Ironically, this approach might even be considered a kind of *harmonization*, in that it attempts to make sense of contradictions, though not by explaining them *away*. I am trying not to defend the text as the unerring Word of God but simply as the product of competent and creative writers.

*

It might prove helpful to do a little advance briefing about the four Gospels and their authors' agendas because this will give us insight into why they may have made some of their changes. Mark's Gospel seems to have been the first one, the first one surviving at any rate. In important ways, Mark is the simplest Gospel. There are places where, compared to the others, he seems theologically more "primitive." He is untroubled by the notion of Jesus lining up with the sinners for John the Baptist's ritual of repentance. The subsequent evangelists (Gospel writers) are increasingly uneasy about it. He does not mind Jesus being unable to heal people who did not believe in him. He has no nativity story to tell, nor any depiction of resurrection appearances. And yet Mark is anything but unvarnished reporting. As William Wrede showed, he has constructed his Gospel around the elaborate premise of the Messianic Secret, which colors his entire narrative like dye permeating cloth.[3] He also maintains an extensive polemic against the twelve disciples, a fossil of forgotten early Christian factionalism.

Matthew used so much of Mark that his Gospel could justifiably be called a revised edition of Mark. But whereas Mark appears to lean toward Paulinism or even Marcionism in its

---

[3] William Wrede, *The Messianic Secret.* Trans. J.C.G. Greig (Edinburgh: James Clarke, 1905).

antipathy toward the twelve, Matthew venerates them as the figureheads of the Christian faith he knows. Rather than rejecting Mark as some heretical screed and consigning it to the flames, Matthew preferred to "correct" and rehabilitate the earlier Gospel. He improves the depiction of the disciples. He has Jesus (anachronistically) take an anti-Pauline position, vis-à-vis the Jewish Torah, to the point of depicting Jesus as a new Moses and his teaching as a new Pentateuch. Matthew appears to have been writing from the multi-lingual, multi-ethnic congregation in Antioch or perhaps Galilee. He regards his Christianity as the best kind of Judaism and in fact seems to be a Jewish scribe representing a movement competing with so-called Formative Judaism as headquartered at Yavneh (Jamnia) following the Jewish War against Rome.

Because of the diversity in his church(es), however, much like what we see in the Epistle to the Romans, the Gospel of Matthew appears to contain materials representing competing factions within the author's own community. Not only so, but this Gospel is like a great tree with visible rings attesting its growth: we can discern at least two "Matthean" redactors. The first is the one who revised Mark, who improved the image of the twelve. The second is someone who took the twelve back down a peg, moving back somewhat toward Mark's version, especially concerning Peter. It is admittedly complicated but not necessarily confusing.

Luke also saw Mark as too good to reject completely. So he, too, used most of it, though not quite as much of it as Matthew did. He joins Matthew in polishing the tarnished image of the twelve. But Luke is not a partisan of Torah-Christianity. Instead, he is writing from the standpoint of what is called "early Catholicism." High on Luke's agenda is the reconciliation of Jewish and Pauline Christianities. He either advocates such reconciliation or presupposes it. Perhaps even higher on Luke's list is his suppression of the fervid apocalyptic enthusiasm of an earlier generation. As Hans Conzelmann demonstrated, Luke and its sequel, the Acts of the Apostles, pursue an intricate and systematic program of realignment.[4] For Luke, there is no longer any point in expecting the imminent end of the age. Promises of its early occurrence have been disappointed (more than once), and it is time to "get real." Luke does not see history as about over but as ongoing. Luke's Jesus does not announce the any-moment dawning of the End. Rather, he inaugurates a new and potentially lengthy epoch, the Church Age. The End will come someday, sure, but not any time soon. In the meantime, Christians must be about their Jesus-assigned duties. The Church (and it is, at this point, proper to start capitalizing it) has become the Institution of Salvation, her apostles (and, more importantly, their successors, the bishops) dispensing grace and the assurance of salvation.

John's Gospel has a decidedly gnostic flavor. Though the author (I think) knew the other Gospels, he obviously did not feel inclined to reproduce their texts with any close accuracy because he has a rather different story to tell. Unlike the Jesus depicted in the other Gospels, the Johannine Jesus virtually ignores the keynote theme of the Synoptics (i.e., Mark, Matthew, and Luke), namely the kingdom of God. Instead, this Jesus promises "eternal life," *here and now*. Nor is his focus the loving heavenly Father but rather Jesus' own role as divine Revealer—whose principal revelation is that he *is* the Revealer. As Rudolf Bultmann points out, John seems to quite clearly eliminate any futuristic eschatology, the expectation of a future return of Jesus.[5] John's "second coming" is Jesus' resurrection, which seems almost synonymous with the post-Jesus coming of the Paraclete, the Spirit of Truth, who will dwell within believers. This radical revision of Christian belief gets obscured by someone (the "Ecclesiastical Redactor") who deemed all this heretical nonsense but dared not simply excise it from the widely-read text and who therefore resorted to adding new material that restored traditional conceptions.

---

[4] Hans Conzelmann, *The Theology of St. Luke*. Trans. G. Buswell (New York: Harper & Brothers, 1960).

[5] Rudolf Bultmann, *The Gospel of John: A Commentary*. Trans. G. R. Beasley-Murray, R.W.N. Hoare, and J.K. Riches. (Philadelphia: Westminster Press, 1971), p. 261.

And this brings up one more type of complication in the interpretation of the Gospels. There are, as I have already anticipated, clear signs of such "ecclesiastical redaction" in all the Gospels, attempts by scribes and editors to align the Gospels with emerging second-century orthodoxy. We have seen that this process already began when, for example, Matthew made changes to Mark. It continued in the efforts of pre-canonical ecclesiastical redactors and even later as copyists tinkered with the texts.[6]

I know this is a lot to keep straight, but I believe the result will be not confusion but, rather, elucidation as we proceed. The individual cases to be examined here will illustrate these general assertions, and, reciprocally, these preliminaries should allow those subsequent studies to make sense more easily. I sure hope so!

Robert M. Price
Festivus 2020

---

[6] Bart D. Ehrman, *The Orthodox Corruption of Scripture: The Effect of Early Christological Controversies on the Text of the New Testament* (New York: Oxford University Press, 2011).

1

Biography

Where Was Jesus Born?

Does it matter? Probably not to us—except, ironically for the nuisance caused by the Nativity narratives of Matthew and Luke. It's not that the two gospels posit different candidates for Jesus' birthplace; rather, they agree he first appeared in the town of Bethlehem ("House of Bread") but tell very different tales of how it happened. Both evangelists (gospel writers) were trying, each in his own way, to square a contradiction between the fact that Jesus was known as "the Nazarene" (or the "Nazorean," both of which spellings occur in the gospels, with the popular belief that the Jewish Messiah would be born in Bethlehem). Would not "the Nazarene" imply he was instead from Nazareth?

Why, you may ask, did anyone think he was supposed to have been born in Bethlehem? Because of an over-literal reading of Micah 5:2–4:

> But you, O Bethlehem Ephrata, who are little to be among the clans of Judah, from you shall come forth for me one who is to be ruler in Israel, whose origin is of old, from ancient days. Therefore he shall give them up until the time when she who is in travail has brought forth; then the rest of his brethren shall return to the people of Israel. And he shall strand and feed his flock in the strength of [Jehovah], in the majesty of the name of [Jehovah] his God. And they shall dwell secure, for now he shall be great to the ends of the earth.

This passage originally served not as a predictive prophecy but was more of a *pro forma* oracle announcing great hopes for either a newborn heir to the throne of Judah or, just as likely, for the reign of a newly inaugurated king of Judah.[1] Others like it have been preserved in Psalms 2 and 110; Isaiah 9:6–7 and chapter 11. I say "over-literal" because the mention of Bethlehem probably is intended as metonymy for the Davidic dynasty, David having been born in Bethlehem. It is just like calling a king "the root of Jesse" (Isa. 11:1), since Jesse was David's father. Thus Micah 5:2 did not mean to say the king in question need himself hale from Bethlehem, only that, unlike the kings of Israel to the north, the king of Judah belonged to the ongoing dynasty of David.

How did the verse come to be interpreted as referring to a future super-king, the Messiah? Once the Judean monarchy was swept away by the conquest of Judah by Nebuchadnezzar's Babylonian armies, Jews began to pin their hopes on a Davidic king who would one day cast off the oppressors and restore Jewish sovereignty. Accordingly, they started applying these birth/enthronement oracles to that future Deliverer, taking them to be predictions of that king. Matthew figured that Jesus was that prophesied king, so he simply assumed, as most of his Christian brethren did, that Jesus was born in Bethlehem. So did Luke, though he does not happen to cite the Micah text.

Was there any more reason to think Jesus was born, or even later dwelt, in Nazareth? Many critical scholars dismiss Bethlehem as a gratuitous inference from Micah 5:2 and then just default to Nazareth as Jesus' birthplace. But that is equally problematic, and for a pretty big reason: there is no definitive evidence that the location of Nazareth was actually inhabited at the time. It had a long history of settlement, but there is a conspicuous absence of relics definitely datable to the first third of the first century CE.[2] Mainstream scholars tend not to take this problem into account and blithely go on assuming there was a Nazareth Jesus could have lived in. So how did Jesus come to bear the epithet "of Nazareth"? Actually, the English translation is unwittingly misleading. Jesus is

---

[1] Sigmund Mowinckel, *He That Cometh: The Messiah Concept in the Old Testament and Later Judaism*. Trans. G.W. Anderson (New York: Abingdon Press, 1954), pp. 103–124.

[2] Rene Salm, *The Myth of Nazareth: The Invented Town of Jesus* (Cranford: American Atheist Press, 2008). Mainstream "experts" do not try to refute Salm except by sneering at his work.

called "Jesus the Nazarene" or "Jesus the Nazorean." A town named Nazareth is mentioned in Luke 4:16 as Jesus' hometown, but the parallel accounts in Mark 6:1–6 and Matthew13:53–58 lack the name, speaking only of "his own country."

It looks like what happened was that "Jesus the Nazarene/Nazorean" originally tagged Jesus as a member of "the sect of the Nazarenes" (Acts 24:5), a group that already existed among Jews in pre-Christian times. The epithet meant "the keepers," i.e., of the Torah, or of the secrets (cf. 1 Cor. 4:1: "stewards of the mysteries of God"). They made their living as itinerant carpenters (cf. Mark 6:3, "Is not this the carpenter?").[3] But Christians came to feel it improper that the Son of God should have been one more member of a pietistic sect, since for them Jesus himself had become the center of religious devotion (cf. the demotion of John the Baptist in Matthew 3:13–14 and 11:11). So they redefined "Nazarene" as "resident of Nazareth." As it happened, Nazareth had once again been inhabited after the ostensible lifetime of Jesus but before the evangelists were writing, so they simply stipulated that Jesus originated there.

So where are we? Matthew and Luke agree (albeit with no factual basis) that Jesus was born in Bethlehem but later lived in Nazareth. But how each gets to his conclusion is very different. As David Friedrich Strauss showed long ago, Matthew imagines that Mary and Joseph lived in Bethlehem until an angel tipped Joseph off about King Herod's impending slaughter of the town's infants and toddlers, directing them to take refuge in faraway Egypt.[4] When Herod died, the angel told Joseph that the coast was clear, so they packed up the station wagon and headed for home. But, on second thought, the angel returned and commanded a change in plans: Herod's son and successor, Archelaus, was a chip off the old block and might still pose a danger to the Holy Family, so they had

---

[3] Hugh J. Schonfield, *The Passover Plot: New Light on the History of Jesus* (New York: Bantam Books, 1967), "North Palestinian Sectarians and Christian Origins," pp. 199–206.

[4] David Friedrich Strauss, *The Life of Jesus Critically Examined.* Trans. George Eliot (Mary Ann Evans). Lives of Jesus Series (Philadelphia: Fortress Press, 1972), pp. 152–156.

better relocate up north in Nazareth of Galilee, which they did. *Voila!* Born in Bethlehem, lived in Nazareth!

Luke, on the other hand, did not think of that. He pieced it together in a whole different way. According to him, Mary and Joseph lived in Nazareth but had to travel down to Bethlehem in order to register for Roman taxation since everyone had to sign up, not where they actually lived, but rather where their remote ancestors had once lived! And while they were there, Mary's time came, and the stork dropped off Baby Jesus, after which they returned home to Nazareth.

Everything renders this story implausible (because impossible): first, a Roman taxation census would not have extended to cover Judea (where Bethlehem was located) since Judea was still technically independent of Rome, albeit a client state (like the Warsaw Pact nations were to Soviet Russia in the twentieth century). Second, no census requires people to register where their ancestors lived instead of at their own address. The tax collectors want to know where to find *you*, not them. Third, Luke refers to the census being ordered by Quirinius, Roman governor of Syria, and while there *was* in fact such a census, it took place in 6 CE, when, according to Matthew's version, Jesus must have been ten years old!

It is obvious that the two Nativity stories face each other in nearly entire contradiction. How did this happen? From what I have already said, it is pretty apparent that Matthew and Luke were both, well, making it up as they went along. From a fundamentalist viewpoint, this is even worse than a simple error. It is literary creation, as both authors were trying to replace ignorance with best-guess speculation. If you are looking for solid information, you are not going to find it in these stories. But maybe you're being too picky! You need to follow Rudolf Bultmann's advice: if your initial question finds no answer in the text, it is likely you're asking the *wrong* question.[5] Go back to the drawing board and revise your question. This time you may hit pay dirt. But if not,

---

[5] Rudolf Bultmann, "Is Exegesis without Presuppositions Possible?", Trans. Schubert M. Ogden. In Ogden, ed., *Existence and Faith: Shorter Writings of Rudolf Bultmann* (Living Age Books/Meridian Books/World Publishing, 1960), pp. 289–296.

keep trying, back and forth till, you get your aim right and you find the answer the text wants to give. In this case, as in several others we will look at, you start seeking history, but you eventually realize the texts are giving you literature instead. That seems disappointing only if you insist the Bible be something it's not.

Misquoting Micah?

Remember that quote from Micah?   Matthew does not quite reproduce the text accurately. His citation of it reads, "And you, O Bethlehem, in the land of Judah, are *by no means* least among the rulers of Judah; for from you shall come a ruler who will govern my people Israel" (Matt. 2:6). What's the difference, you ask? Micah noted the irony that, despite its humble insignificance, sleepy little Bethlehem will produce a great king to rule the nations. But Matthew is writing as a Christian who believes that this Messianic ruler has come, and that his advent has conferred a greater dignity upon Bethlehem. Matthew cannot help himself: he rewrites the Micah verse, inserting into it the fulfillment of it! What makes this rather minor inconsistency loom large if you are in the inerrancy business? One biblical writer claims he is quoting another biblical writer, but he tampers with it.

But as evangelical scholar Everett F. Harrison reminds us that we have no right to demand that biblical writers adhere to anachronistic modern standards of accuracy.[6] Often they are just not even playing the same game we are. The Targums were paraphrases of books of the Hebrew Scriptures for Jews who did not know Hebrew but had come to speak Aramaic instead. But they were not simple, literal translations like the Syriac (North Aramaic) Peshitta. The Targums were more akin to modern works like *The Living Bible*, interpretive paraphrases that vary frequently and significantly from the originals. The Targumists were only trying to convey what they took to be the intention of the original authors, but, as modern translators know only too well, it is often difficult to draw a firm line between translation and interpretation

---

[6] Everett F. Harrison, "Criteria of Biblical Inerrancy." In Frank E. Gaebelein, ed., *Christianity Today* (New York: Pyramid Books, 1968), pp. 86–90.

and, even commentary: "Let me make it a bit clearer for today's readers…" The result was that the Targums were the Scriptures all right—as the Targumists read and understood them. Similarly, the Jewish historian Josephus, introducing his book *Antiquities of the Jews*, promised his readers he would tell the story of biblical history straight, neither adding nor omitting anything. But you quickly realize he has casually veered off his course. He is relating the Bible story all right, but as he had read and remembered it. He was not trying to pull the wool over anyone's eyes. Neither was Matthew. Not accurate by our standards, but perfectly legitimate for him.[7] To understand this does not oblige the modern reader to believe what the biblical writer said; it just absolves that writer of the charge of chicanery.[8]

Miraculous Mis-conception?

The issue for us here is not the possible factual nature of this theo-mythical claim. No, our task is to weigh up contradictions in the texts, historically accurate or not. It must be noted that, according to Jane Schaberg, it is not completely clear that either Matthew or Luke is really trying to tell us that Jesus was the product of a miraculous conception with no human father. It is possible, when you compare Matthew 1:18 with Targumic versions of Genesis 38:24–26, that Matthew's "to be with child by the Holy Spirit" (Matt. 1:18) just *might* mean that, even though Mary was raped or seduced, God was nonetheless redeeming her shame by using it as the occasion of the Incarnation. Similarly, when Matthew quotes Isaiah 7:14 ("Behold, a virgin shall conceive…") he may not have meant a woman innocent of sex, since the Greek word

---

[7] Krister Stendahl, *The School of St. Matthew and its Use of the Old Testament* (Philadelphia: Fortress Press, 1969), pp. 39–46; Richard Longenecker, *Biblical Exegesis in the Apostolic Period* (Grand Rapids: Eerdmans, 1975), "Jewish Hermeneutics in the First Century," pp. 19–50; Barbara Thiering, *Jesus the Man: A New Interpretation from the Dead Sea Scrolls.* (Transworld Publisher/A Corgi Book, 1993), "The Pesher Technique," pp. 28–35.

[8] Joseph A. Wheless, *Is It God's Word? An Exposition of the Fables and Mythology of the Bible and of the Impostures of Theology* (New York: Alfred A. Knopf, 1926), pp. 283–284.

("*parthenos*") he found in the Septuagint and used (Matt. 1:23) may not have been so strict in meaning but had come to bear the same ambiguity as the Hebrew *almah*, "young woman."[9] This no doubt sounds contrived, but Schaberg's argument is fine-tuned and not without force.

Similarly, Luke 1:34 ("How shall this be since I know not a man?"), the only indication of a virginal conception in Luke, appears to be a clumsy interpolation by some scribe who was alarmed not to find the virgin birth contained in the Lukan Nativity and decided to supply what was lacking. Note how the protest of Mary interrupts the canticle of the angel Gabriel, something that never happens in the Lukan canticles ascribed to Mary (Luke 1:46–55), Zechariah (Luke 1:68–79), and Simeon (Luke 2:29–32, 34b–35).[10] Luke 2:5 calls Mary Joseph's "betrothed," but even as his fiancée she could still be legitimately pregnant since in their culture betrothal was not exactly equivalent to our status of engagement. Divorce was necessary to break the betrothal agreement, and the betrothed couple were allowed to cohabit. Besides, some manuscripts have "his wife" instead of "his betrothed," apparently because a scribe was aware that they amounted to pretty much the same thing (or perhaps to avoid implications of scandal).

But for the sake of argument, let us assume both evangelists *did* mean to affirm a virginal conception. In that case, we find a glaring clash between this and the two genealogies, both of which trace Jesus' messianic lineage back to King David via Joseph, a Davidic descendant. *But what is the point if Joseph was not Jesus' father?* Apologists and conservative scholars say, as if they believed it, that Joseph in effect *adopted* Jesus, who could

---

[9] Jane Schaberg, *The Illegitimacy of Jesus: A Feminist Theological Interpretation of the Infancy Narratives* (San Francisco: Harper & Row, 1987), "Matthew's Account of Jesus' Origin," pp. 20–77.

[10] One might point out that Simeon's song *is* interrupted by the stage direction in verses 33–34a, but it is necessary in order to swivel the narration from Simeon's address, first to God, then to Mary.

therefore lay claim to Joseph's Davidic pedigree.[11] I can only say this seems absurd on the face of it. You can easily imagine the laughter such a claim would invite. "Hosanna to the *adopted* son of David!" This would never pass muster. The issue, after all, was the royal *bloodline*. The only way I could see this is if we posited that Jesus was begotten by some brother of Joseph (Pandera?), and that this brother died before *his* son Jesus was born. Then Joseph, in accordance with the Levirate marriage law whereby, in order to keep property in the family, the surviving brother would beget offspring for the newly widowed mother, his sister-in-law, though he need not marry her (Deut 25:5; Mark 12:19). But the son would be the legal heir of the dead dad. The story as we read it says nothing of the kind.

Since the logic of the gospel genealogies demands that Jesus be Joseph's son, we have to infer that either subsequent scribes added them to the Nativity stories, using as paste the contrived-sounding qualifiers "the husband of Mary, of whom Jesus was born" (Matt. 1:16b) and "being, as was supposed, the son of Joseph" (Luke 3:23a). Each is a sudden jog in the road; neither naturally belongs. But it might not have been a scribe who was the culprit. It might have been Matthew himself, trying to harmonize a genealogy he got from somewhere (or that he had created) with the virgin birth tradition. Ditto with Luke or a later scribe.

The Gospel of John, interestingly, features no Nativity story at all and seems to assume that Joseph was Jesus' natural father, since he has a disciple say so without correction (John 1:45). Similarly, John has someone in the crowd come mighty close to denying Jesus' birth in Bethlehem on the grounds that the Messiah will one day appear as if from nowhere, but that Jesus' origin is well known. And where might that be? Presumably Galilee, as in 7:52, where a Sanhedrinist pontificates that, since "no prophet is supposed to rise from Galilee," Jesus, being a Galilean, cannot possibly be the Christ. Again, there is no attempt

---

[11] Raymond E. Brown, *The Birth of the Messiah: A Commentary on the Infancy Narratives in Matthew and Luke.* (Garden City: Doubleday, 1977), pp. 138–139.

by the narrator to inject a disclaimer, and he actually has Jesus accept the premise but reject the conclusion: "You know me, and you know where I have come from" (John 7:28).

The situation is basically the same in Mark. His gospel has nothing at all to say of Jesus' birth, much less its location. On top of that, he seems, on any fair reading, to have Jesus scoff at the very idea that the Messiah is supposed to be a descendant of David:

> Why do the scribes say the Christ is the son of David when David himself, inspired by the Holy Spirit, declared, "The Lord [Jehovah] said to my Lord [King Messiah], 'Here, sit at my right hand till I put your enemies under your feet.'" David himself calls him Lord, so how can he be his son? (Mark 12:35–37)

Jesus assumes, as did his contemporaries, that David authored Psalm 110 and that, in accord with traditional filial piety, a father would never recognize one of his own sons as his lord (cf. Genesis 37:10: "His father rebuked him, and said to him, 'What is this dream that you have dreamed? Shall I and your mother and your [older] brothers indeed come to bow ourselves to the ground before you?'"). It is cringe-worthy to witness the gymnastics of harmonists, beginning perhaps with Matthew (22:42), to make the passage mean something else: "Oh, he meant to say that the Christ *is* the son of David but much more besides! He is the Son of God!" Nice try. Instead the saying must stem from Galilean Jews or Christians whose forbears had long before repudiated the house of David: ("What portion have we in David? We have no inheritance in the son of Jesse. To your tents, O Israel! Look now to your own house, David!" (1 Kings 12:12:16b). Morton Smith suggests that Mark may have been oblivious of the implications of this anecdote and included it just because he wanted to show Jesus outwitting his foes.[12] But it does seem to preserve the fact that not everyone expected (or even *wanted*) a Davidic Messiah.

---

[12] Morton Smith, *Jesus the Magician* (San Francisco: Harper & Row, 1978), p. 170: Such anecdotes "are told to show his cleverness in escaping traps."

Generating Genealogies

What are we to conclude from these flagrant contradictions? That the gospels are worthless hackwork? Hardly! Instead we should appreciate the fact that, even if their authors had to juxtapose incompatible materials, in this way they had preserved precious (because fascinating) bits of ancient traditions in the manner, not of a consistent narrative, but of a scrap book. But what if the genealogies were original compositions by the evangelists? The choices are not restricted to "hoax or history" as we sometimes hear. Why do you think there are professional genealogists? The fact presupposes that few people are in possession of complete family records going all the way back to the beginning of the family line. That is why people pay them to research scraps of information from recondite sources unknown or unavailable to the common person. Like all historical reconstructions, the resultant family tree charts are necessarily hypothetical because inevitably conjectural. If all the links between the generations were readily recoverable, we wouldn't be going to the professional! I am suggesting that this is what the two gospel genealogists were doing, namely their best, and with no real evidence except names from the Bible who might be plausible candidates for messianic ancestors. It would have been total speculation in their case, but they apparently thought they were making the necessary connections to link Jesus to David on the dogmatic assumptions that Jesus was the Christ and that the Christ (contra Mark 12:35–37) had to be Davidic.

Which one is the genuine article? Neither. Luke's is festooned with various Levitical (priestly) names incompatible with Davidic descent. Matthew 1:12 names King Jeconiah as a member of the royal line culminating in Jesus (actually Joseph!). But Jeremiah had disqualified any and all descendants of that king from ever inheriting the throne (Jer. 27:20). Oops! Now *that's* a goof pure and simple. There *are* some. But this one would imply that Jesus was a false messiah—if anyone noticed it.[13]

---

[13] Someone might at this point want to invoke the Criterion of Embarrassment and argue that a forger of the messianic family tree would not

We are not finished with the genealogies yet. Forget the forest for a moment and take a closer gander at the trees. The lists of names are completely incompatible once you get past David, whereupon Luke traces Jesus' (Joseph's!) descent through the line of Nathan, while Matthew traces it through a different son of David, Solomon. The usual dodge is to say that Luke is really giving us *Mary's* family tree, not Joseph's, because wives' genealogies were always subsumed under those of their husbands! There was, however, no such ridiculous custom. Of course this is merely a reflection of the ruse that Jesus was the adopted son of Joseph. In both fanciful cases it is posited that the genealogies of both Jesus and Mary have been omitted or were unknown, so that of Joseph was appropriated for both!

But if that harmonization is patently laughable, it pales in comparison to the solution offered by Rudolf Steiner, the founder of Anthroposophy, who proposed that there were *two different Jesus children*, one descended from David via Nathan, the other via Solomon! Eventually the Nathan Jesus boy died and his spirit entered the body of his Solomonic counterpart![14] One might dub this astonishing Christology "Super-Nestorianism." Nestorius was said to have believed Jesus harbored two persons within him, one divine, one human. But Steiner's Jesus is a multiple personality!

---

have made such an error, so it must be an authentic genealogy, But that need not follow. Since when are forgers necessarily inerrant?

[14] "Steiner reveals in Jesus of Nazareth the union of two human streams, the sinless nature of the New-Adam, and the fullest and richest development of human nature through all the millennia of its reincarnating development. In so doing he gives the deepest significance to those seemingly contradictory elements in the nativity stories of the gospels of S. Matthew and S. Luke, which are for the most part disregarded or explained away, and which, interpreted materialistically, are the grounds on which rational modernism disputes the truth of the recorded events." A.P. Shepherd, *Scientist of the Invisible: Rudolf Steiner* (Rochester, VT.: Inner Traditions International, 1983), p. 135–136. Also, Bernard Nesfield-Cookson, *The Mystery of the Two Jesus Children and the Descent of the Spirit of the Sun* (Forest Run: Temple Lodge Publishing, 2005); Rudolf Steiner, *Lectures on the Gospel of St. Luke.* Ten Lectures given in Basle 15th–26 September 1909. Trans. D.S. Osmond with Owen Barfield (London: Rudolf Steiner Press, 1964), "The Two Jesus Children," pp. 126–144.

Emmanuel Can't

Finally, have you ever noticed that, while Matthew 1:21 has an angel instruct Joseph to name his son "Jesus" (Matt. 1:21), the following Old Testament proof text, Isaiah 7:14, concludes with, "'his name shall be called Emmanuel' (which means, God with us)"? Which is it? Of course he is henceforth called Jesus. What is going on here? It is on one level a contradiction, but if you read to the end of the book you will find the risen Jesus assuring the disciples that "I am with you always, even to the consummation of the age" (28:20). For Matthew, this promise counts as the fulfillment of Isaiah 7:14's prophecy about Emmanuel. The correspondence he intends is not between the *names* "Emmanuel" and "Jesus," but rather between the promise implicit in "Emmanuel"(namely that "God is *with us*") on the one hand and, on the other, Jesus' Great Commission promise that he will be *with the apostles* as they go forth to evangelize. Implied here is even the possible identification of the risen Christ with God himself! Here is a contradiction that turns out to be a revelation *par excellence*.

After All I've Tried for Three Years,
Feels Like Thirty, Feels Like Ninety

How many years did Jesus' ministry last? We always hear that Jesus was publicly active for three years. This estimate is based on the number of Passover celebrations mentioned in the Gospel of John, namely three, the first at John 2:13, 23; the second at 6:4; and the third at 11:55; 12:1; 13:1; 18:28, 39; 19:14. Since we cannot tell how long before the first one Jesus' ministry began, we don't know whether John envisioned a two-year ministry (beginning with the first Passover and ending at the third) or a three-year career. But scholars admit that the events narrated in the Synoptic gospels (Matthew, Mark, and Luke) seem to imply no more than a single year of public activity. It might be too much to call this difference a contradiction. It is not unreasonable to ascribe it to differing (but unknown) selection interests underlying the traditions employed in the Synoptics versus John.

But if we *should* consider the disparity a contradiction, we have a case analogous to that of the Pauline mission itinerary depicted in Acts as opposed to that implied in the Pauline epistles. John Knox[15] and others have demonstrated that the two implied sequences cannot be harmonized, and that the Acts version is an artificial schema, one of various possible attempts to structure the various traditions earlier circulating independently (e.g. 1 Thess. 1:7–9). The data from the epistles do not fit easily into the three missionary journeys recounted in Acts. Likewise, John's schema appears to be arbitrary as to any actual order of events but instead results from a theological agenda. John has three Passover-relevant things for his Jesus character to say and do; hence he needs to construct three Passover scenes in which Jesus may say and do those three items.

This seems to be clear from John's placing of the Temple Cleansing at the *start* of Jesus' ministry instead of at the *end* of it as in the Synoptics. As Bultmann[16] pointed out, John has structured the story as one long Passion narrative, spreading it back over the whole gospel. If he had instead actually stated that Jesus cleansed the temple at the beginning instead of toward the end, as in the Synoptics, we would indeed have a contradiction, and the usual harmonization, that Jesus did it twice, would be laughable. He couldn't have gotten away with it *twice* since he didn't get away with it *once*!

This is also why there is all the talk of "witness(es)" (John 1:7–8, 15, 32, 34; 2:25; 3:11, 26, 28, 32; 5:31–39; 8:13–18; 10:25; 12:17; 15:26–27; 18:23) and "testimony" (John 1:7, 19; 3:11, 32–33; 4:39; 5:32–36; 8:13–17; 19:35; 21:24), as well as the repeated attempts to execute Jesus (John 5:17; 7:1, 19, 25; 8:37, 40, 59; 10:31–33; 11:8). The trial of Jesus before the Sanhedrin fills the whole gospel! John, then, is constructed thematically, not strictly chronologically. The disparity between John and the Synoptics is not some error but marks the difference between two ways of

---

[15] John Knox, *Chapters in a Life of Paul* (New York: Abingdon Press, 1950).

[16] Rudolf Bultmann, *The Gospel of John: A Commentary*, Trans, G.R. Beasley-Murray, R.W.N. Hoare, and J.K. Riches (Philadelphia: Westminster Press, 1971), p. 644 plus fn 3.

presenting Jesus. Otherwise, why even have more than a single gospel in the first place?

Similarly, how do we "harmonize" the conflicting dates for the Last Supper? Matthew, Mark, and Luke place it on Passover, while in John it takes place the night before. Yes, technically, one version must be factually inaccurate, but it was no stupid goof. Clearly John has pushed the Supper back one day in order to be able to depict Jesus' death as coincident with the slaughter of the Passover lamb on the Day of Preparation (John 19:31). The point is the same as in 1 Corinthians 5:7: "Christ, our paschal lamb, has been sacrificed." This is why John cites Exodus 12:46 ("No bone of him shall be broken") at the crucifixion—it deals with preparation of the Passover lamb. And think of John the Baptist's characterization of Jesus as "the Lamb of God who takes away the sin of the world" (John 1:29).[17] Anyone who frets over the "inconsistency" between John and the Synoptics on this point is "straining out a gnat and swallowing a camel" (Matt. 23:24).

The Old Age and the New Age

How old was Jesus when he died? Thirty-three, right? Uh, not necessarily! The common opinion is the sum of adding Luke 3:23 plus the three Passovers in John. Luke estimates that when Jesus went public, he was "about thirty." If we take John literally (which I have already tried to show is a mistake), that adds another three years, though, like his fellow Synoptists, Luke implies only a single year of activity, so maybe we shouldn't just combine Luke and John.

Besides, there is a fascinating alternative tradition. Irenaeus claimed that Jesus was a half-century old when he was crucified! Accordingly, he died in the reign of Claudius, not earlier, under Tiberius. Where did Irenaeus get this? From the Gospel of John. Following Jesus' demonstration in the temple, the authorities

---

[17] We must note that originally the Passover sacrifice was not supposed to be an atonement for sin but rather a commemoration or celebration of the liberation from Yul Brynner in Egypt. Does this oddity imply that the New Testament writers were actually ignorant of the religious culture they supposedly shared?

demand to know what gave him the right to disturb the peace. He replies, "Destroy this temple, and in three days I will raise it up!" Typically, John has Jesus' critics stupidly misunderstand him: "It has taken forty-six years to build this temple, and will *you* raise it up in three days?" John comments: "But he spoke of the 'temple' of his body" (John 3:18–21). Let us see: add the *forty- six* years to the *three* days and you get forty-nine…of *something*, but it is the number itself that matters. Later, in John 8:56 Jesus boasts that Abraham had a prophetic vision of Jesus and his deeds, but Jesus' idiot detractors take his words in the stupidest possible way, as if he means he is eighteen hundred years old! "You are not even fifty years old, and you have seen Abraham?" (John 8:57). This would seem to imply that Jesus was closer to fifty than to forty. Otherwise, it would surely make their point more effectively to say, "You're not even *forty* yet, whippersnapper!" And remember, in John's gospel, the crucifixion occurred at the third Passover, which means the Johannine Jesus died at age forty-nine![18] But of course, and chronology based on John's symbolic pseudo-chronology is a house built on sand.

---

[18] Alfred Loisy, *The Gospel and the Church*. Trans. Christopher Home (1903; rpt. Lives of Jesus Series. Philadelphia: Fortress Press, 1976), p. 33.

2

John the Baptist

Was John Elijah?

John the Baptizer is usually considered to be Jesus' forerunner. He paved the way for Jesus as he who should unleash a baptism of Spirit and fire. But this is true in another sense, too. The John character can be understood as a literary prototype for the Jesus character. There are parallels between the two that throw light on both once we start comparing them. For instance, if there is a puzzling ambiguity in the gospels over whether Jesus considered himself to be the Messiah, there is similar confusion over whether John saw himself as the (figuratively) returned Elijah. Did Jesus accept and affirm Peter's confession of faith in him as the Christ (Mark 8:27–31; Matt. 16:13, 20–22; Luke 9:18–22)? Mark seems to imply that he did, but that he immediately redefined the messianic role as that of the suffering Son of Man—and he warned the disciples not to blab his secret to the press (so to speak). This complicates things nicely! If Jesus totally redefined the messianic role, is it even meaningful to say he accepted the designation "Messiah"? It seems like a question of mere semantics. He is not making it easy for theologians to do their Christologies! Likewise, when asked point blank by the Sanhedrin, Jesus returns a maddeningly ambivalent answer: "You have said so" (Matt. 26:64) or "I am" (Mark 14:62, though some few manuscripts have "You say") or "You say that I am" (Luke 23:70). Huh? Does he mean "You said it!" or "If you say so"? Before Pontius Pilate, when asked essentially the same question Jesus says, "You have said so" (Matt. 27:12; Mark 15:2; Luke 23:3) or "You say that I am a king" (John 18:37). Pilate seems to hear this as a big yes since he goes on to pronounce sentence on Jesus as a seditionist would-be king (Matt. 27:37; Mark 15:26; Luke 23:38; John 19:19). On this basis many scholars[1] conclude that, yes, Jesus did deem himself the Jewish Messiah, but that does not really settle it. Bultmann[2] and others point to seemingly adoptionist passages like Romans 1:4 ("designated/declared Son of God…by his resurrection from the dead") and Acts 2:36 ("God has made him Lord and Christ, this Jesus whom you crucified"; cf. Acts 13:30–35). How could any Christians have said such things if they knew Jesus had claimed to be the Messiah already before the crucifixion? I have to think Wrede[3] was right, and that the texts that imply Jesus' own messianic self-consciousness were the products of Christians growing weary of waiting for Jesus to return as Messiah and decided to "messianize" his first coming, the only coming available. And this means it was early Christians, not Jesus, who redefined "Messiah" in terms of redemptive suffering and death.

Do we not see the same kind of thing going on in the gospels' sketch of the Baptizer? Did John think he was a latter-day Elijah? He is conspicuously dressed like Elijah, wearing a hair shirt (2 Kings 1:8; Mark 1:6), but on the other hand Zechariah 13:4 implies this was the common garb of *all* ostensible prophets. So we cannot be sure John was wearing an Elijah Halloween costume; instead, he may have been simply wearing the traditional prophet uniform.

Jesus is said to have pegged John as the neo-Elijah in Mark 9:11–13 and Matthew 17:10–13. Though Luke omits that remark, elsewhere he ascribes to an angel an Elijah-John connection: "he will go before him in the spirit and power of Elijah" (Luke 1:17). Does this mean that John *is* Elijah? Not quite. Not necessarily. Did Luke mean to substitute this statement about John for the one he found in Mark 9:11–13? Mark did not just come out and say John was Elijah returned, but that is surely in implication, as Matthew saw: "Then the disciples understood that he was speaking to them

---

[1] Nils Alstrup Dahl, *The Crucified Messiah and other Essays* (Minneapolis: Augsburg Publishing House, 1974), pp. 10–36.

[2] Rudolf Bultmann, *Theology of the New Testament.* Trans. Kendrick Groebel. Scribner Studies in Contemporary Theology (New York: Scribners, 1951), p. 27.

[3] William Wrede, *The Messianic Secret.* Trans. J.C.G. Greig (James Clarke, 1905).

of John the Baptist" (Matt. 17:13). Matthew says as much again in Matthew 11:13–15: "For all the prophets and the law prophesied until John; and if you are willing to accept it, he is Elijah who is to come. He who has ears to hear, let him hear." Luke has the same saying about the Baptist as the object of ancient prophecy (Luke b 16:16), which is therefore a saying from the Q source he shared with Matthew, but Luke has again omitted the equation of John with Elijah." It looks as if Luke was not too keen on John being understood as Elijah.[4] Why would this be?

Hans Conzelmann[5] provided the answer that is a bit complicated in its own right. Conzelmann, one of Bultmann's doctoral students,[6] marked out a complex but compelling Lukan schema whereby *Heilsgeschichte* (sacred history) falls into three great dispensations. First is the period of *Israel*. Obviously this includes the Old Testament but continues through the first two chapters of Luke's gospel.[7] John the Baptist is the capper of it, the last of the prophets (analogous to Muhammad, the ostensible Seal of the Prophets)—but *not* the returned Elijah. John prepares the way for Jesus to begin the second dispensation, the all-too-brief era of the Messiah. John himself does not belong to it. This Jesus-period begins, not with Jesus' birth, but with his baptism, which of course inaugurates his ministry. Most of this time Conzelmann denominated the "Satan-free" period, when the devil has retreated after Jesus' victory in the wilderness temptations: "And when the

---

[4] You might say the question was whether John and Elijah were *homoousias* or *homoiousias*.

[5] Hans Conzelmann, *The Theology of St. Luke*. Trans. Geoffrey Buswell (New York: Harper & Row, 1960).

[6] I am grateful to be even a minor part of this apostolic succession, as my *Doktorvater*, Darrell J. Doughty, was a student of Hans Conzelmann, Bultmann's disciple, who in turn was Adolf Schlatter's disciple.

[7] Actually, Conzelmann thought these two chapters were post-Lukan additions, but I think the whole *Heilsgeschichte* framework discerned by Conzelmann is the work of the Ecclesiastical Redactor, probably Polycarp of Smyrna, who added the Catholicizing passages to the original Marcionite "Luke" to create our canonical Luke. See David Trobisch, *The First Edition of the New Testament* (New York: Oxford University Press, 2000); Trobisch, "Who Published the New Testament?" *Free Inquiry* 28/1 (December 2007/January 2008), pp. 30–33.

devil had ended every temptation, he departed from him until an opportune time" should present itself (Luke 4:13). He will return when he enters the disgruntled Judas (Luke 22:3) to engineer the betrayal of Jesus. But in the meantime Satan is banished, bound so that Jesus may despoil him of his possessions, i.e., the poor wretches afflicted by demon-possession, as he does throughout the gospel narrative. Once that period is over, Jesus smells the ozone before the coming storm and tells the disciples to prepare themselves: "And he said to them, 'When I sent you out with no purse or bag or sandals, did you lack anything?' They said, 'Nothing.' He said to them, 'But now, let him who has a purse take it, and likewise a bag. And let him who has no sword sell his mantle and buy one'" (Luke 22:35–36).

The third dispensation is the Church age. Here the apostles take over and administer the Church as the Institution of Salvation and the Custodian of Orthodox Truth. This is also "the times of the Gentiles," including the Gentile Mission. Loisy put it perfectly: "Jesus foretold the kingdom, but it was the Church that came."[8] Conzelmann explained that Luke was writing when the eager expectation of the Second Coming was a thing of the past, so long had it been delayed, and Luke realized Christians had better settle down for the long haul. Yes, Jesus will return someday, but not tomorrow. This is what Ernst Käsemann, another brilliant Bultmann disciple, called "nascent Catholicism."[9]

Conzelmann's adjustment of apocalyptic categories into church-historical categories is evident in his treatment of the "Satan-free period." What he sees Luke doing there is to "demythologize" the scenario of Revelation 20:1–3:

Then I saw an angel coming down from heaven, holding in his hand the key of the bottomless pit and a great chain. And he

---

[8] Loisy, *Gospel and the Church*, p. 166.

[9] Ernst Käsemann, "Paul and Early Catholicism." Trans. Wilfred F. Bunge. In Käsemann, *New Testament Questions of Today* (Philadelphia: Fortress Press, 1969), pp. 236–251; Eric Franklin, *Christ the Lord: A Study in the Purpose and Theology of Luke-Acts* (Philadelphia: Westminster Press, 1975); Martin Werner, *The Formation of Christian Dogma*. Trans. S.G.F. Brandon (Boston: Beacon Press, 1965).

seized the dragon, that ancient serpent, who is the Devil and Satan, and bound him for a thousand years, and threw him into the pit, and shut it and sealed it over him, that he should deceive the nations no more, till the thousand years were ended. After that he must be loosed for a little while.

The Gospel of John shares with Luke-Acts a large number of direct and indirect parallels, one which is the denial that John the Baptist was Elijah:

And this is the testimony of John, when the Jews sent priests and Levites from Jerusalem to ask him, "Who are you?" He confessed, he did not deny, but confessed, "I am not the Christ." And they asked him, "What then? Are you Elijah?" He said, "I am not." "Are you the prophet?" And he answered, "No." They said to him then, "Who are you? Let us have an answer for those who sent us. What do you say about yourself?" He said, "I am the voice of one crying in the wilderness, 'Make straight the way of the Lord,' as the prophet Isaiah said." (John 1:19–23)

Is Conzelmann really saying much more than that? Sometimes you need a complex explanation to understand a simple thing. Likewise, we can already see Conzelmann's claim about the demotion of the Baptist summed up in the Q saying Matthew 11:11, "Truly, I say to you, among those born of women there has risen no one greater than John the Baptist; yet he who is least in the kingdom of heaven is greater than he." Compare Luke 7:28, virtually the same verse verbatim. Personally, I am convinced that the first half of the saying originated in the sect of John the Baptist before their Christian competitors co-opted it, adding the second half in order to subordinate the Baptizer not only to Jesus but even to the most insignificant *schlemiel* in the (Christian) kingdom of God.[10]

---

[10] And, between you and me, I could supply a couple of nominees for that position.

Albert Schweitzer offered an ingenious harmonization of John and Mark/Matthew on this point that should not go unmentioned. He theorized that John the Baptist believed Jesus to be Elijah, "him who is to come," but that Jesus thought instead that he himself was the Messiah and that John, though he did not realize it, was Elijah, his forerunner.[11]

A Face in the Crowd

Did John the Baptist recognize or endorse Jesus as the Messiah? It depends on which gospel you are reading at the moment. Mark's gospel, the oldest one we have, has Jesus show up for John's baptism, but it gives no hint that John knew Jesus from Adam. To him, Jesus was just one more *schmuck* confessing his sins (which were presumably pretty trivial).[12] The Q source depicts John wasting away in Herod's dungeon when it suddenly occurs to him to dispatch a couple of disciples, still at liberty unlike their master, to ask Jesus if he might be the one whose imminent advent he had announced (Matt. 11:2–3/Luke 7:18–20). This bit fits Mark better than it does the two gospels that borrowed it from Q. That is, it is reports of Jesus' fantastic miracles that prompts John's question. It's as if he had not heard of Jesus before, until these intriguing reports reached him. John's hopes are raised! Maybe God's victory is at hand at last, and John will soon be set free! Of course he is not going to be that lucky. But apologists and sermonizers invariably tell it quite differently, as if John had already settled on Jesus as the Messiah, but that his initial enthusiasm had begun to wane. If this guy was really King Messiah, what the hell was John doing sitting here in the dark, fending off rats and wishing for a toilet? The text gives no hint of any of this.

In fact, just the opposite; would news of your guy performing miracles be likely to *disappoint and discourage* you? Of course not! Instead, if you *had not* thought the Messiah had yet

---

[11] Albert Schweitzer, *The Mystery of the Kingdom of God: The Secret of Jesus' Messiahship and Passion.* Trans. Walter Lowrie (1914; rpt. New York: Schocken Books, 1964), p. 149.

[12] Remember: as Kant explained, it is only the righteous who repents, because he is the one with a conscience! The real reprobate doesn't give a damn.

appeared, this news would ignite your hopes![13] The usual reading is the worst kind of far-fetched harmonization. The "disappointed John" version is the only way inerrantists and apologists can think of to square the story with Matthew 3:13–15 and John 1:29–30 where (though these two accounts differ in all other respects) the Baptizer publicly acknowledges and endorses Jesus. But this is merely to read the Q story as if it were connected with the baptism story, which it is not. Obviously, Matthew's gospel does contain both, but there is no effort to reconcile them with each other. It is just what John C. Meagher called "clumsy construction."[14] Matthew *could* have simply omitted the prison episode, but he found it useful to affirm that Jesus had performed the deeds predicted by Isaiah for the Messianic age (cf. Matt. 11:5 with Isa. 35:5–6; 61:1).

Now how about the Matthean and Johannine endorsement stories? They are, as I say, quite different except for the endorsement itself. Indeed, there are whopping differences. In Matthew, John the Baptist knows Jesus for what he is as soon as he sees him at the head of the line (excellently depicted in Scorcese and Schraeder's *The Last Temptation of Christ*, with John portrayed by a wizened Andre Gregory). And he does not want to baptize him! "*I* need to be baptized by *you*! And *you* come to *me*?" Jesus succeeds in persuading the flabbergasted prophet. Jesus seems to be saying it is mainly for show: "It is fitting for us to fulfill all righteousness," i.e., every pious gesture, as when stolid citizens go to church because that is what stolid citizens do. I guess. But it does not really matter *what* Matthew intends; he just wants to relieve his readers' unease at the idea of Jesus showing up to a baptism for the remission of sins, something that did not seem to cause Mark to lose any sleep. But as time (and redaction) went on, this became a ticklish issue. There were two embarrassing problems. First, the notion of Jesus having had sins and, worse yet, remission of sins. Second, if Jesus goes to John for ministry, and not the other way around, who comes off looking like the superior

---

[13] Strauss, *Life of Jesus*, p. 222.

[14] John C. Meagher, *Clumsy Construction in Mark's Gospel: A Critique of Form- and Redaktionsgeschichte*. Toronto Studies in Theology Volume Three (New York and Toronto: Edwin Mellon Press, 1979).

figure? Billy Graham or some *schmo* who comes forward at his altar call? Matthew did not feel at liberty to completely rewrite Mark's original story, so he just added to it. But the evangelist John was more daring: he omits the baptism completely! Yet, for him, John endorses Jesus nonetheless!

> And John bore witness, "I saw the Spirit descend as a dove from heaven, and it remained on him. I myself did not know him; but he who sent me to baptize with water said to me, 'He on whom you see the Spirit descend and remain, this is he who baptizes with the Holy Spirit.'" (John 1:32–33)

This is not just different from Matthew's version, it contradicts it, since Matthew has the Baptizer recognize Jesus as soon as he sees him, before he immerses him, while John's gospel, though it says nothing about Jesus getting wet, does say John recognized Jesus only once he saw the Spirit descend upon Jesus, something that happens in the Synoptics only after Jesus comes ashore. The Gospel according to the Ebionites goes even farther: Jesus' mother hears about John "doing his baptism thing"[15] and suggests the whole family make the trip to get dunked and saved. Spoilsport Jesus objects: "What sins have I committed that I should need baptism?"

What is going on here? The whole thing arose from a continuing rivalry between the movements of Jesus and of John. Once Jesus came on the scene, John's group continued conspicuously to go their own way. According to Luke 11:1, John had taught special prayers to his disciples. Mark 2:18 tells us John's followers practiced fasting and wondered why Jesus' followers did not.[16] If John had actually endorsed Jesus as the Messiah (just as Akiba would later endorse Simon bar Kochba), can we imagine John would have maintained his sect at all? Would he not retire and direct his followers to join Jesus? John's gospel has him do exactly that:

---

[15] Tim Rice, *Jesus Christ Superstar*. MCA Records, 1970.

[16] Joseph Klausner, *Jesus of Nazareth: His Life, Times, and Teaching.* Trans. Herbert Danby (New York: Menorah Publishing, 1979) pp. 248–249.

> The next day again John was standing with two of his disciples; and he looked at Jesus as he walked, and said, "Behold, the Lamb of God!" The two disciples heard him say this, and they followed Jesus. (John 1:35–37)

But John's gospel itself provides most of our reason for believing in an ongoing competition between the John and Jesus sects. The evangelist stresses again and again that, apparently, *someone* thinks John was the Light of the world (John 1:8), that John was the Christ (1:20, 3:28–30). Similarly, Luke is at pains to have the Baptist deny that he is the Messiah, contrary to the belief of some. The fourth-century Pseudo-Clementines actually record a debate between Christians and Baptists in which the Baptist spokesman points out that John was Jesus' superior since *he* baptized *Jesus* and not the reverse (sound familiar?). They pointed out that, if Jesus said John was the greatest man ever born of women, this must mean he acknowledged John's superiority over himself, so why do Christians not? John's devotees affirmed that John, not Jesus, was the real Messiah.

Why would they have kept going after Herod Antipas had his head chopped off? Here is why: in Mark 6:14 we read that some were already preaching that the martyred John had risen from the grave, newly empowered with divine energy to perform miracles. Mark assumes such beliefs were mistaken interpretations of Jesus' own miracles, but that is only his attempt to debunk a rival sect. "John the Baptizer has been raised from the dead; that is why these powers are at work in him" (Mark 6:14). This was, I think, the resurrection kerygma of the John the Baptist sect. Note the similarity to the Christological slogan preserved in Romans 1:3–4: Jesus was "descended from David according to the flesh, and designated Son of God in power according to the spirit of holiness by his resurrection from the dead."

I cannot blame any reader who may think that my multi-jointed attempt to sort out the disparate, puzzling bits of gospel texts bearing, in this case, on John the Baptist is itself a clever harmonization in order to connect the dots into a structure that will allow all of them to make sense together. As such, is it any better than the contrivances offered by fundamentalists to vindicate the Bible from accusations of error and contradiction? Am I not just going to a lot of unnecessary trouble to get to the same conclusion?

But I think I am not. The fundamentalist is trying to carry off the pretence that these inconsistencies are illusions when in fact they are not. My job is to show *why* they *do* contradict one another. I am trying to vindicate the texts by making their phenomena understandable, refusing to drive them, square pegs, into the round holes of this or that theological system. Surely you can see the difference?

Did Jesus Wait in the Wings?

Mark implies that Jesus waited till John was out of the way to begin his own preaching campaign: "Now after John was arrested, Jesus came into Galilee, preaching the gospel of God, and saying, 'The time is fulfilled, and the kingdom of God is at hand; repent, and believe in the gospel'" (Mark 1:14–15). "Now when he heard that John had been arrested, he withdrew into Galilee; and leaving Nazareth he went and dwelt in Capernaum by the sea" (Matt. 4:12-13). Luke says that Herod Antipas "shut up John in prison" (Luke 3:20), then relates the baptism of Jesus in a flashback, leaving an open door of ambiguity as to whether it was actually John who baptized Jesus (3:21), and only in 4:14 does Luke have Jesus begin preaching. But John's gospel goes its own way, *all* the way. In this gospel, Jesus' ministry is well underway while John is yet free (John 3:24), and eventually we even hear that there is a competition between Jesus' own baptismal ministry and John's, with Jesus' group pulling out ahead (John 4:1–3)!

> Now when the Lord knew that the Pharisees had heard that Jesus was making and baptizing more disciples than John (although Jesus himself did not baptize, but only his disciples), he left Judea and departed again to Galilee.

This just does not fit into the Synoptic picture at all! But many scholars, even critical scholars, try to integrate this bit into their historical Jesus constructions. Suppose Jesus undertook an initial period of apprenticeship with the Baptist, a disciple of

John's just as Peter, Andrew, and the rest would later be to him.[17] Perhaps they divided up the candidates for baptism in order to process them more quickly. But Jesus eventually came to part ways with his mentor, presumably because John was still waiting for the kingdom of God and Jesus came to believe the kingdom had snuck up on them and was just waiting for someone to recognize it—and that someone was none other than Jesus! Thus the competition. It would have been the very first denominational schism in Christian history! In John 3:25–30 one of the Baptist's assistants approaches him and expresses his dismay at Jesus' success at John's expense. "He's top of the poll!"[18] But John reassures him all is well, all is going according to plan. John's time is drawing to a close, and he's starting to sound like Paul in Philippians!

But right here we find another contradiction: if John had already proclaimed Jesus as the awaited savior and even advised his own disciples to switch their allegiance to Jesus as Andrew and another actually did (John 1:35–37), *why is he continuing his own ministry?* This is like the episode of the old *Andy Griffith Show* when Sheriff Andy has missed the deadline for filing to run for re-election, and Deputy Fife first decides to seek the job himself with Andy's blessing, but then convinces Andy to allow him to head up a write-in campaign for him. At first Barney plans to drop out of the election but then agrees it is better for the town to have a two-man race, so he will run a sham campaign just as a formality. But his ambition gets the better of him, and he hires a sound truck to advertise his candidacy and even bad-mouths Andy at a public debate! Soon he thinks better of it and endorses Andy after all. This is all very funny, but in John's gospel it is not supposed to be! So what is going on here?

Remember, for this gospel, chronology is at the service of theology and is as flexible as the writer needs it to be. This whole business is strategically anachronistic, placing on stage the bitter rivalry between early Christians and the ongoing John the Baptist

---

[17] Bruce Chilton, *Rabbi Jesus: An Intimate Biography* (New York: Doubleday Image. 2000), "The *Talmid* of John," pp. 41–63.

[18] Rice, *Jesus Christ Superstar.*

sect. The point is to appropriate the figure of John in order to have "John" tell his latter-day followers, those in the gospel-writer's day, to be good and give way to the Jesus sect. "It is what John would have wanted! In fact, er, it is what he *did* want, see?"

Another clue is the notice in John 4:2 that Jesus himself did not baptize anyone. That's a wink to the reader: this did not really happen when Jesus was on earth. The fact that it is his disciples who are doing the dunking is a tip-off, if you are willing to accept it, that the competition described here really belongs to a later, post-Jesus, time. Indeed it is the perfect example of Bultmann's axiom[19] that stories in which the practice of the disciples is criticized, not that of Jesus himself, means that the story arose in the context of the early church, not the ministry of Jesus, as in Mark 2:18, 23–24; 7:1–2; 9:17–18.

What did He Say and to Whom did He Say It?

It is not every day you hear a voice from heaven. In fact, unless you are a paranoid schizophrenic, it is not *any* day you hear a voice from heaven! But there was a day, according to the Synoptic gospels, when Jesus did hear one. Of course, this event climaxed his baptism in the Jordan. But there are certain inconsistencies between the accounts of Matthew, Mark, and Luke (and between all of them and John). Otherwise we would not be discussing them here! Let us start with Mark, in all probability the earliest surviving gospel. Mark depicts Jesus, dripping wet, coming up out of the water and on to the river bank, when "*he* saw the heavens opened and the Spirit descending into him like a dove; and a voice came from heaven, "*You* are my beloved son; with *you* I am well pleased" (Mark 1:10–11). This is not a historical report, no one's memory. Rather it is a literary creation. Why? Because the divine utterance has been cobbled together from Psalm 2:7 ("You are my son; today I have begotten you"), Isaiah 42:1 ("Behold my servant, whom I uphold, my chosen, in whom my soul delights, and I have

---

[19] Rudolf Bultmann, *The History of the Synoptic Tradition.* Trans. John Marsh (New York: Harper & Row, 1968). p. 16.

put my Sprit upon him") and Genesis 22:2 ("Take your son your only son Isaac, whom you love.., and offer him... as a burnt offering"). God is quoting God! In other words, Mark wants the line he feeds to the Almighty to *sound* like God. What attracted Mark to these particular passages of scripture? Just look at the sections he did not quote but to which he implies reference: there we have the anointing with the Spirit and the hint of a coming sacrifice of a beloved son. Get it? Mark hoped you would, and now you do.

It is clear that this whole thing is to be viewed as experienced by Jesus alone. The voice speaks to *him*, no one else, and he is the only one to see the skies parting and, accordingly, the descent of the dove. Why is Jesus the only one who is aware of all this? Presumably because this is how Jesus *becomes* God's son, or at least becomes *aware* that he is God's son. The former seems more likely Mark's intention, since this must be the difference made in Jesus by the Spirit when it merges with him. This is certainly the way certain adoptionist and Gnostic readers of Mark read it. I think they were right.

But Matthew did not. Here is his version: "Behold, the heavens *were opened* and he saw the spirit of God descending like a dove and *alighting on* him; and lo, a voice from heaven, saying, '*This is* my beloved son, *with whom* I am well pleased'" (Matt. 3:16). This time, though only Jesus is said to see the descent of the dove, it says simply that the heavens *were opened*, i.e., objectively, for all to see. Likewise, the voice speaks *not* to Jesus, but to *the crowd*. Not "you are," but "this is." Why? Because *Jesus already knows*. Mark has no Nativity story, but Matthew does. So, for him, Jesus must have known his true identity ever since childhood.

Now Luke. "[When] Jesus also had been baptized and was praying, the heaven was opened, and the Holy Spirit descended upon him in bodily form, as a dove, and a voice came from heaven, 'You are my beloved Son; with you I am well pleased" (Luke 3:21–22). Some manuscripts replace the second clause with "today I have begotten you," i.e. the continuation of the "You are my Son" decree of Psalm 2:7. I am persuaded that this is the original Lukan text, and that the majority of copies represent a scribal harmonization, adjusting Luke to Mark. Maybe the scribe intentionally "corrected" Luke, or perhaps he just absent-mindedly assumed Luke read the same as Mark—who knows?

Why would Luke have restored the original line from Psalm 2? It was originally sung as an enthronement hymn to celebrate the new king's accession to the throne of Judah. Luke must have had some idea of this, and judged it appropriate here because he elsewhere gives new emphasis to the ascended Jesus reigning from heaven, not just acting as our mediator with his Father (e.g. Acts 7:56; cf. 2 Macc. 15:12–16, where both Jeremiah and the martyred high priest, Onias III, occupy such a position in heaven, interceding for the Jews). Earlier on, Christians had expected the imminent return of Jesus to take up his millennial reign over the nations, but he turned out to be a no-show. So, like the Millerites and Jehovah's Witnesses would do nearly two thousand years later, they decided Jesus must have begun his reign after all, but *invisibly, in heaven.*[20] In this way, Luke sought to reassure persecuted Christians who were feeling abandoned and considering throwing the whole thing over.

But there is another alteration of Mark's original. Like Matthew, Luke appears to have been aghast at Mark's Gnostic adoptionism implied in the descent of the Spirit "into" Jesus, so he did the same thing Matthew did, changing "into" to "upon."

There is no heavenly voice in John's gospel, at least none that the public heard. Rather, God's (or an angel's?) voice whispered to John the Baptist, "He upon whom you see the Spirit descend and remain, this is he who baptizes with the Spirit" (John 1:33b). Then John, in turn, tells the crowd, "I saw the Spirit descend like a dove from heaven, and it remained on him" (John 1:34). Why this change? Because, again, the evangelist John extends Jesus' trial retroactively through entire gospel, and is therefore calling the Baptizer as a witness for the defense: hence in this very passage, John says "I have seen and have borne witness that this is the Son of God" (John 1:34; 5:33–35).

And, in case you had not noticed, John's gospel does not ever say Jesus got baptized! Did he take it for granted? No, I think he suppressed it. We have already seen how Matthew, Luke, and

---

[20] Eric Franklin, *Christ the Lord.*

the Ebionite gospel tried to mitigate the Christological embarrassment occasioned by Mark's original at this point, and John's gospel just says, essentially, "The hell with it!" He cuts the Gordian Knot instead of wasting time trying to unravel it.

The Devil on Jesus' Shoulder

There is perennial debate over whether Matthew and Luke used Mark and a now-lost document that we call "Q" (for *Quelle*, German for "source"). Some think Matthew used Mark and then Luke used both Matthew and Mark. Still others believe Matthew had Mark and Luke, who had used Mark, in front of him. Either way, you could account for Matthew and Luke sharing material not found in Mark.[21] But I am an old mossback and still find the Q hypothesis quite cogent. I will not pursue this further here, except that it is marginally relevant to our investigation. Scholars point out that Q was almost entirely made up of sayings or micro-stories issuing in saying of Jesus. These "pronouncement stories" posit some context to provide an occasion to help make the saying intelligible.[22] But there is a fly in the ointment, namely the Temptation narrative. You see, it is a *narrative!* Otherwise, Q doesn't really have any.

But I believe the Temptation story was not part of Q. You see, it was lacking in Marcion's copy of Luke (or what would eventually be called Luke). I accept the judgment of Tübingen scholars like Gustav Volkmar, F.C. Baur, and Albrecht Ritschl that Marcion by no means snipped out passages from Luke that he found theologically distasteful, but that someone added these very passages to the original form used by Marcion. It seems plain to me that the Temptation narrative is one more Matthean creation on the basis of Old Testament texts, in this case, Deuteronomy. As all recognize, the first diabolical temptation (Matt. 4:3–4) is based on Deuteronomy 8:3. Temptation two (Matt. 4:6–7) is based on

---

[21] Congratulations! No more mysteriously vanished "Q" source. But, uh, now you have a non-extant source that either Matthew used to supplement Mark *and* the vanished source of information Luke used to beef up Matthew! Or the other way around. Good luck with *that*.

[22] Rudolf Bultmann, *History of the Synoptic Tradition*, p. 47.

Deuteronomy 6:16. The third one (Matt. 4:8–10), comes from Deuteronomy 6:13–15. But what is usually ignored is that the element of Satan showing Jesus all the earth's kingdoms and offering them to him has to be directly based on Deuteronomy 34:1–4, where Moses climbs up to the peak of Mount Nebo,[23] where God shows him all the territory that his Israelites will conquer and occupy. This sort of thing was Matthew's stock-in-trade (Matt. 13:52). It is not Q-ish material. So how come we find it in Luke? It was borrowed from Matthew by the redactor who padded out the Marcionite gospel. (I believe it was the same man who added material to the originally Gnostic Gospel of John, whom Bultmann dubbed the Ecclesiastical Redactor, most likely to be identified as Polycarp of Smyrna).

Interestingly, Mark did not have such a story. He did have Jesus retreat to the desert following his baptism to be tested by Satan (just as, e.g. Job and David were), but there is no mention of three distinct encounters with the devil. Nor does Mark give the impression that Jesus fasted the whole time; instead, angels fed him as they had Elijah in 1 Kings 19:4–8.

Why is the order of the Matthean/Lukan Temptations different between the two gospels? Scholars debate whether it was Matthew or Luke who changed Q's, but on my reading, the answer is clear: Luke's redactor borrowed them from Matthew, so Matthew's was the original order. The third Temptation was the offer of the kingdoms. So why did the Lukan redactor place that one second? Possibly he wanted to end with the notion that, though Jesus might be tempted to have God's angels rescue him *from the cross*, as Satan suggested God would have them protect him from a headlong fall from the pinnacle of the temple, Jesus would not take the easy way out. It might be viewed as equivalent to Matthew 26:53–54: "Do you think that I cannot appeal to my Father, and he will at once send me more than twelve legions of angels? But how then would the scriptures be fulfilled, that it must be so?" Also, think of Matthew's version of the Caesarea Philippi confession, where Peter reproves Jesus for the latter's prediction of his own

---

[23]A mountain named, ironically, for Nebo, one of the alien deities Jehovah tells Moses to command the Israelites not to worship!

crucifixion: "God forbid, Lord! This must never happen to you!" (Matt. 16:22). Jesus disdainfully replies, "Get behind me, Satan!" (Matt. 16:23).

3

The Disciples

Names on a List

The three Synoptic gospels contain lists of the twelve disciples (Mark 3:16–19; Matt. 10:2–4; Luke 6:14; cf, Acts 1:13). John 21:2 gives only a partial list, and that only in an appendix subsequently tacked on. The lists do not match precisely. Why not? Mark names a "Thaddaeus," which most manuscripts of Matthew repeat, while others substitute the name "Lebbaeus." Some copies have "Lebbaeus called Thaddaeus," which is obviously the contribution of some puzzled scribe, comparing two different copies of Matthew, one with "Lebbaeus," the other with "Thaddaeus;" he figured he had best harmonize them. And fundamentalists keep trying. Luke knows nothing of either "Thaddaeus" or "Lebbaeus," but *does* have a "Judas of James," i.e. "son" or "brother of James." John's gospel concurs, with its "Judas not Iscariot." So harmonists contend that this Judas was also Mark's Thaddaeus under yet another alias. They *have* to. I believe Walter Schmithals [1] was right in thinking the group of twelve was a post-Jesus development. Somebody else, someone within Jewish Christianity, came up with the notion of a council of twelve to mirror the twelve tribal patriarchs of tribal Israel, perhaps emulating the governing structure of the Qumran sect. As for our lists, who knows *where* they came from? My guess would be that a subsequent generation compiled a list of great "apostolic" names of the past. But there were too many nominees, so one faction championed a man named Thaddaeus, another rooting for Lebbaeus, yet a third for Judas of James, and differently aligned scribes inserted the names of their favorites.

---

[1] Walter Schmithals, *The Office of Apostle in the Early Church*. Trans. John E. Steely (Nashville: Abingdon Press, 1969), pp. 68–71.

Perhaps Cephas was another, and so they combined Peter with this Cephas.

But the strangest puzzle is that of Levi and Matthew. No list includes a "Levi" among the twelve (unless perhaps "Levi" is a short form of "Lebbaeus"?), and all include Matthew. The trouble is that Mark has a scene in which Jesus recruits a tax collector named Levi and celebrates with him and his IRS colleagues at his house. Matthew repeats the story with but one change: now the tax man's name is *Matthew*! Neither gospel has "Matthew also called Levi" or anything like that. And if you compare the actual lists in Mark and Matthew you find that, whereas Mark had, simply, "Matthew," the Gospel of Matthew has "Matthew the tax collector." The evangelist we call "Matthew" must have wondered why Mark included a perfectly good "calling" story without including the character among the twelve. It sounded just like the calling stories starring Peter and Andrew, James and John, after all. But no Levi among the twelve? It *is* surprising. But the Matthean writer decided to cut Levi out and give his fifteen minutes of fame to the disciple Matthew instead. So Matthew becomes both a disciple *and* a tax agent at the same time—through a stroke of the evangelist's pen.

Haven't We Met Before?

Of most of the disciples we never learn anything but their names. Not even in the Acts of the Apostles! Peter (and of course Judas) is an exception. He is essentially a literary figure, playing Doctor Watson to Jesus' Sherlock Holmes. His dumb questions are devices to allow "Jesus" to explain things for the reader's benefit. But why so much *nothing* about the others? This would be quite natural if the apostolic names are actually those of later church bureaucrats. There would be nothing to report about them that would make sense occurring in the time and circumstances of Jesus.

The "calling" stories seem to be "ideal" (i.e., artificial) examples for the reader, to make him or her vicariously feel the summons to Christian discipleship and to heed it.[2] We can well

---

[2] "He comes to us as One unknown, without a name, as of old, by the lake-side, He came to those men who knew Him not. He speaks to us the same word: 'Follow thou Me!' and sets us to the tasks which He has to fulfil in our

imagine there was more than one story of, say, Peter's call to follow Jesus. Actually the gospels give us *three*. Mark has the classic version in which Jesus suddenly appears on the shore of the Lake of Galilee to two groups of brothers, all fishermen, and issues his summons: "Follow me and I will make you fishers for men!" They have never set eyes on him before, but they instantly drop what they are doing and leave their fathers to shoulder the family business. Though there are no miracles attached to Mark's story of the disciples' summons, it is, I think, the most powerful of all. These nondescript men, living undistinguished lives, suddenly hear the voice of Destiny calling them to something of momentous import. They recognize the moment and step boldly into the future.

But this was not good enough for Luke. No, he decided there had to be more to it. What could have convinced these guys to react in such a radical manner? It must have been a miracle, a literal one! So in Luke Peter does a stranger a favor, rowing Jesus out a short distance from shore so he can address the crowd without getting pressed into the surf by enthusiastic fans. After dismissing the audience, Jesus thanks Peter by conjuring up a huge shoal of fish for them and their partners. Then he tells Peter, "Follow me." Can we reconcile this with Mark's version? "Well, it happened as Luke said, but Mark did not think the fishy feat worth mentioning." Really?

No, Luke just did not think Mark's story was plausible, so he tried to improve it, ruining it in my opinion. But at least we know why the two incompatible versions exist. Paradoxically, Luke felt the need to rationalize Mark's story, albeit by the expedient of a miracle!

But it gets even more complicated. The Johannine Appendix (John chapter 21) has another version. This time it is a resurrection appearance. Seven of the disciples are out in the boat fishing just before dawn, and suddenly a lone figure shouts from shore: "How's the fishing, lads?" The nets are trailing, all empty, until Jesus, like

---

time. He commands. And to those who obey Him, whether they be wise or simple, He will reveal Himself in the toils, the conflicts, the sufferings which they shall pass through in His fellowship, and, as an ineffable mystery, they shall learn in their own experience Who He is." Albert Schweitzer, *The Quest of the Historical Jesus: A Critical Study of Its Progress from Reimarus to Wrede.* Trans. W. Montgomery (1906; rpt. New York: Macmillan, 1968), p. 403.

Aquaman, summons a school of fish to fill the nets. One of the disciples understands and breathlessly whispers, "It is the *Lord*!" Back on dry land, a dripping Peter reaffirms his loyalty to Jesus, presumably ashamed of having earlier denied him, and then Jesus calls Peter to "Follow me" (John 21:19). This time he makes Peter a shepherd of men rather than a fisher for men, but what is the difference?

I think that the Lukan version was originally a resurrection story, too. Jesus meets the disciples fishing there, too, but *they already know him*. Thus they are there with rod and reel because, disillusioned by the crucifixion, they have called it quits and returned to their secular jobs. And when in Luke's retelling, we can now see what Peter was talking about when he said, "Depart from me, O Lord, for I am a sinful man!" *He must be referring to his recent denials*. And this must be what Jesus is referring to in John 21 when he asks three times, "Peter, are you *sure* you love me?"

Finally, in the first chapter of John, we witness a scene in which, contra Mark, Jesus meets Andrew and Peter already before the arrest of John the Baptist. In fact, Andrew was one of the two disciples of John who left the nest to follow Jesus at the Baptizer's own urging. In this case, when Jesus calls Peter and Andrew to dump the nets and follow him, they must already have been acquainted with him. Trying to square this with Mark's version just overwrites and really nullifies Mark's. And that is what always happens in harmonizing contradictions: you just create a mishmash that obscures the distinctions intended by each. If you do this, you are pretty much admitting that you are not interested in the Bible for its own sake, but only as a hostage to your favored theology.

Confession and Omission?

The favorite passage of Roman Catholics is Matthew 16:17–19:

> And Jesus answered him, "Blessed are you, Simon Bar-Jona! For flesh and blood has not revealed this to you, but my Father who is in heaven. And I tell you, you are Peter, and on this rock I will build my church, and the gates of Hades shall not withstand it. I will give you the keys of the kingdom of heaven, and

whatever you bind on earth shall be bound in heaven, and whatever you loose on earth shall be loosed in heaven."

Why do we find this passage only in Matthew's gospel? If Jesus really said this, why does it not occur in Mark, Luke, or John? Were they just economizing on ink? Running out of space? No, it was a matter of public relations. I believe Arlo J. Nau[3] has correctly deconstructed the tradition. We start with Mark's Caesarea Philippi episode (8:27–33) in which Peter correctly surmises the true identity of Jesus: "You are the Christ" and receives only the charge not to tell anyone else. But as Jesus goes on to redefine the messianic role as that of a suffering sacrifice (or something), Peter does not like what he is hearing and presumes to correct Jesus, who in return calls poor Pete "Satan" and tells him to get the hell away from him! Yikes! This accords with Mark's general ill-treatment of the disciples.[4]

Both Matthew and Luke manifest the opposite tendency and often retell stories so as to mitigate Mark's apostle-antipathy and to rehabilitate the twelve. Mark's perspective was practically Marcionite, painting the twelve as a bunch of blockheads who never understand Jesus.[5] But his fellow Synoptists represent a more Catholic-leaning view, venerating the saintly founders of Mother Church. Thus Luke omits Jesus' stunning rebuke to Peter altogether. Matthew, in rewriting Mark, probably originally did the same, only to have a subsequent redactor pop the Petrine balloon his Matthean predecessor had inflated. You see, Matthew's gospel was very likely written in Antioch, where, according to Galatians, Peter and Paul both had followers, though Paul apparently found himself isolated and left.[6] We can still detect tensions between the two apostles and their fandoms.

---

[3] Arlo J. Nau, *Peter in Matthew: Discipleship, Diplomacy, and Dispraise.* (Collegeville, MN: Liturgical Press, 1992).

[4] Theodore J. Weeden, *Mark: Traditions in Conflict* (Philadelphia: Fortress Press, 1971).

[5] This is one of the reasons that some wonder if Mark's gospel actually *was* Marcion's gospel.

[6] See my article "Antioch's Aftershocks: Rereading Galatians and Matthew after Saldarini" in *When Judaism and Christianity Began: Essays in*

The uniquely Matthean blessing on Peter (16:17–19) is the contribution of the Petrine faction in Antioch. It makes Peter the very foundation of the Church, implying the primacy, really, of his apostolic-episcopal successors there (a primacy later usurped by Rome by appeal to the tendentious fiction of a joint founding by both Peter and Paul). Not only that, but the blessing also imitates Paul's claim to have derived his gospel from no human source but rather from a direct revelation from the ascended Christ. Only in Peter's case it was the Father in heaven who bypassed "flesh and blood," revealing the truth directly to Peter. I believe that is called "one-ups-manship." Likewise, 1 Corinthians 3:11 says that "no other foundation can anyone lay than that which is laid, which is Jesus Christ." That is, not Peter.

It would, of course, have been one of these Antiochene Paulinists who restored Jesus' rebuke to Peter, albeit in a slightly milder form, without the "Satan" business. He did not think he could get away with just erasing the Petrine blessing (which he must have felt Peter did not deserve), but he could at least "restore some perspective" by restoring the rebuke alongside it.

The first post-Markan Matthean redactor had ascribed to Peter alone the "keys of the kingdom," the rabbinical prerogative of making changes in Jewish practice, as when Johannon ben Zakkai (was said to have) cancelled the red heifer ritual (Num. 19:1–10) and the bitter water ordeal (Num. 5:11–31).[7] But the Paulinist redactor changed this, too, adding a scene in which Jesus commits this privilege to the whole group of apostles in Matthew 18:18, injecting an element of collegiality.[8] (John 20:23 also has Jesus empower all

---

Memory of Anthony J. Saldarini. Volume One: Christianity in the Beginning. Supplements to the Journal for the Study of Judaism Volume 85. Alan J. Avery-Peck, Daniel Harrington, and Jacob Neusner, eds., (Leiden: Brill, 2004), pp. 231–250.

[7] Jacob Neusner, *A Life of Rabban Yohanan ben Zakkai Ca. 1–80 C.E.* Studia Post-Biblica Vol. Six (Leiden: E.J. Brill, 1962), pp. 60–61; Phillip Sigal, *The Halakhah of Jesus of Nazareth According to the Gospel of Matthew.* Society of Biblical Literature Studies in Biblical Literature number 18 (Atlanta: Society of Biblical Literature, 2007), p. 87.

[8] This would have been much the same as the attempt by the Vatican II framers to transfer some of the monarchial authority of the Pope to the bishops. It also seems to underlie the ongoing dispute between the Roman Catholic and

of them to decide whether or not to absolve people's sins, which fits his conspicuous lack of the Caesarea blessing on Peter.)

Peter's confession of faith is a major turning point in the gospel story. But what was it he said? The gospels offer a smorgasbord of Christological confessions. I do not mean to get into the issue of what may or may not have actually occurred; rather, why do the accounts, whether historical or fictional, culminate in different punch lines? Mark's is obviously the simplest. Peter testifies, "You are the Christ" (8:29), the Messiah of Israel. As the ensuing interchange between Peter and Jesus shows, there is still the definition (or *re*definition) of the term to deal with, but here I am interested only in the crucial statement that will invite further clarification. And Peter's is virtually monosyllabic: "Christ."

Luke's version is barely modified: "You are the Christ *of God*" (9:20). Of course, it is God who anointed him ("Messiah/Christ" means "anointed one"). In chapter 4, Luke has Jesus apply to himself Isaiah 61:1, "The Spirit of the Lord is upon me, because he has anointed me," etc.

Matthew 16:16 ascribes to Peter a mini-creed: "You are the Christ, the Son of the living God," which, in accord with Old Testament usage, implies "Son of the true God," i.e., as opposed to the gilded statues worshipped by the foolish pagans. We catch here something of an echo of 1 Thessalonians 1:9–10: "You turned to God from idols, to serve a living and true God, and to wait for his Son from heaven, whom he raised from the dead, Jesus who delivers us from the wrath to come." Matthew, as we have seen, is concerned with the same mission field: the Gentiles (28:19). This is probably why he thus augments Peter's formula: this is what the missionaries from Antioch are to preach to their pagan converts.

One might expect something really spectacular from Peter in John's gospel, given its heavily theological character, but we do not get it. Instead, in John 6:69 Peter says exactly what the demoniacs say in Mark 1:24 and Luke 4:34: "I know who you are, *the Holy One of God*." And it is not as if John has anything against such extravagant affirmations, since he has Nathanael exclaim, early

---

Eastern Orthodox Churches over whether the Pope holds all authority unilaterally or whether he is to be considered "first among equals" with his fellow Patriarchs.

in the story (John 1:49), "You are the Son of God! You are the King of Israel!" Martha of Bethany is no mean theologian, either: "I believe that you are the Christ, the Son of God, he who is coming into the world!" (John 11:27). So what is with Pete? I can only guess what John the evangelist is thinking here. I wonder if he is thinking of Mark 8:33 where Jesus denounces the thick-headed Peter as "Satan" and thus deems the cry of the demons more appropriate from Peter. "Woe is me, for I am lost! For I am a man of unclean lips!" (Isa. 6:5).

With the Gospel of Thomas, we find ourselves on a very different wavelength. The confession scene reads this way:

> Jesus said to his disciples: "Make a comparison to me, and tell me whom I am like." Simon Peter said to him: "Thou art like a righteous angel." Matthew said to him: "Thou art like a wise man of understanding." Thomas said to him: "Master, my mouth will in no wise allow me to say whom thou art like." Jesus said: "I am not thy master, because thou hast drunk, thou hast become drunk from the bubbling spring which I have measured out." And he took him, went aside, and spoke to him three words. Now when Thomas came to his companions, they asked him: "What did Jesus say unto thee?" Thomas said to them: "If I tell you one of the words which he said to me, you will take up stones and throw them at me; and a fire will come out of the stones and burn you up." (Saying 13)

This saying seems to take a Zen-like view of the issue: any attempt to verbalize, to conceptualize, what the Living Jesus is, must create an idol, a poor substitute in his place. The real Jesus, the light shining out from within him, is ineffable. This is why no Christological titles appear in this gospel. Each one carries the baggage of its traditional definition, and the Gnostic Jesus surpasses all of these. This is why Peter gets it wrong this time, because, like Matthew, he ventures an answer to a Socratic question to which there *is* no answer. Incidentally, Matthew's opinion, that Jesus is a philosopher like Socrates or Diogenes, is widely popular among New Testament scholars today, as is Peter's opinion, that Jesus was a theophanic angel.

You Come in Here with a Skull Full of Mush
and You Leave Thinking Like an Apostle

Do the disciples understand the parables? We get two rather different answers. In Mark, it sure seems like they do not. "And he said to them, 'Do you not understand this parable? How then will you understand *any* of the parables?'" (Mark 4:13). I think of two other texts. First, Jesus' eye-rolling disgust: "O faithless generation! How long am I to be with you? How long must I bear with you?" (Mark 9:19). Second, 1 Corinthians 2:14: "The unspiritual man does not receive the gifts of the Spirit of God, for they are folly to him, and he is not able to understand them because they are spiritually discerned." In Pauline terms, the twelve disciples are being portrayed as "unspiritual men." Mark's Jesus expects that they will understand his riddles: "To you has been given the secret of the kingdom of God, but to those outside everything is in parables" (4:11). But they seem still to be no better than outsiders, just as Paul tells the Corinthians, "But I, brethren, could not address you as spiritual men, but as men of the flesh, as babes in Christ."

Matthew does not like this depiction of the disciples, the apostles, so he has Jesus instead give them a star on their homework: "'Have you understood all this?' They said to him, 'Yes.' And he said to them, 'Therefore every scribe who has been trained for the kingdom of heaven is like a householder who brings out of his treasure what is new and what is old'" (Matt. 13:51–52). Just as in the Great Commission Matthew is really addressing his intended readers, the Antiochene missionaries (cf, Acts 13:1–3),[9] not really the eleven apostles he has placed in the scene, even so here, where he gratuitously replaces the numbskull disciples with his own self-characterization as a scribe fully trained and able to expound on both the literal meaning of the Old Testament texts and the new Christian interpretations of them revealed by the Spirit. So, again, the disciples are used as whipping boys by the Paulinist Gospel of Mark,[10] while the apostle-friendly Matthew uses them as exemplars

---

[9] Matthew is hardly alone in using this technique. See Robert M. Fowler, *Let the Reader Understand: Reader-Response Criticism and the Gospel of Mark* (Minneapolis: Fortress Press, 1991).

for Jewish-Christian teachers, whose successor he himself is. Neither portrayal is even really *supposed* to communicate historical information. Both are "written down for our instruction" (1 Cor. 10:11).

The Good Seats

Who has the *chutzpah* to ask for the seats of honor: James and John, *or their mom*? In Mark 10:35–37, the brothers Zebedee work up the nerve to approach Jesus to ask for reservations at the messianic banquet that they expect will shortly be served. When the other ten hear this, they are steamed at James and John (possibly because they wish *they had* thought of it first!). They do not get the answer they want. Jesus tells them it is just not his prerogative to dictate the seating chart. But he does not leave it at that. He brings them up short, asking if they feel they deserve the privilege they desire. Are they capable (or willing?) to join him in his suffering and martyrdom? They better hope so, because that day will come. Will they chicken out? This is quite profound. The scene harks back to that in which Elijah's disciple Elisha, aware, like James and John, that his master is about to leave this mortal coil, makes one last request before it is too late:

> Elijah said to Elisha, "Ask what I shall do for you, before I am taken from you." And Elisha said, "I pray you, let me inherit a double share of your spirit." And he said, "You have asked a hard thing; yet, if you see me as I am being taken from you, it shall be so for you; but if you do not see me, it shall not be so." (2 Kings 2:9–10)

It is a bit more obvious in 2 Kings that Elisha is eager to follow in his master's footsteps as a miracle-working prophet. James and John do want to follow on Jesus' path in the direction they imagine it going, namely enthroned glory, but, like Elijah, Jesus tells them their request is more difficult than they think. It entails the way of the cross. Still interested, boys? It seems they had not yet learned the lesson of Luke 14:7–11:

Now he told a parable to those who were invited, when he noticed how they chose the places of honor, saying to them, "When you are invited by anyone to a marriage feast, do not sit down in a place of honor, lest a more eminent man than you be invited by him; and he who invited you both will come and say to you, 'Give place to this man,' and then you will begin with shame to take the lowest place. But when you are invited, go and sit in the lowest place, so that when your host comes he may say to you, 'Friend, go up higher'; then you will be honored in the presence of all who sit at table with you. For every one who exalts himself will be humbled, and he who humbles himself will be exalted."

Matthew, I think, ruins the original by the simple expedient of inserting Mrs. Zebedee into the frame story (Matt. 20:20–21):

Then the mother of the sons of Zebedee came up to him, with her sons, and kneeling before him she asked him for something. And he said to her, "What do you want?" She said to him, "Command that these two sons of mine may sit, one at your right hand and one at your left, in your kingdom."

Where did *she* come from? Flown in for the occasion? The insertion is clumsy, since Jesus switches from speaking to her to speaking to her sons with no transition at all. In other words, he defaults to the Markan original in mid-sentence. But it is not Jesus who was so rude; it was Matthew. He has lessened the effect of Jesus' reply, since it was James and John whose presumption needs to be rebuked. It is *their* lesson to learn, not that of their blundering stage-mother. Why did Matthew do this? Well, of course he wants to mitigate the shame and the blame due to the "holy apostles." He has confused the point of the story, making it partially and pointlessly parallel to Genesis 27 where Rebecca pushes poor Jacob into hoodwinking his father Isaac to give Jacob the advantage over his big dumb brother Esau. It works but also backfires, which is precisely what the reluctant Jacob had been afraid of! *"Thanks, Mom!"*

4

Jesus' Teaching

Rejected in Nazareth?

All three Synoptics say he was, though only Luke calls the town "Nazareth." John has significantly reworked the tradition but does have a version of it, or maybe an independent parallel to it. But there is a jolting contradiction right in the middle of Mark's version, plus more accumulating with each retelling, so we have plenty to work with!

As the eagle-eyed Bultmann noticed, Mark 6:1–6 is a composite story, clumsily jammed together from two very different pieces. In the first one, verse 1 through most of verse 3:

> He went away from there and came to his own country; and his disciples followed him. And on the sabbath he began to teach in the synagogue; and many who heard him were astonished, saying, "Where did this man *get* all this? What is the wisdom given to him? What mighty works are wrought by his hands! Is not this the carpenter, the son of Mary and brother of James and Joses and Judas and Simon, and are not his sisters here with us?"

The point of this is obviously "Hometown boy makes good." They are praising Jesus, who they had no idea was such a wise sage, much less a miracle-working superman! As far as they knew, the kid was just a carpenter apprenticed to his dad, undistinguished from his many siblings—but *wow!* There is no way to take these acclamations as criticism, but the very next sentence is "And they took offense at him." Huh? *What?* What *happened* here? How did the weather change faster than the time

Jesus stilled the storm? The answer is: it *did not*, not originally, anyway. Not till Mark got ahold of it.

But what *was* the point of this pre-Markan version? There was one. Attention is called to the incongruity between Jesus' humble origins, none of which would have led anyone to expect great wisdom or amazing miracles from him, or the spectacular splash he was making. What could account for this? It is a standard theme in various religious traditions. How could Peter, an untrained Galilean fish-monger, have had the rhetorical skill he displayed before the Sanhedrin (Acts 4:13)? Luke has already told us: he has been filled with the Holy Ghost! How could a dust-caked camel driver, have delivered his prophetic oracles? No surprise if the angel Gabriel was dictating them to him. How could ex-con man and rube Joseph Smith (like Mr. Haney on *Green Acres*) possibly have been capable on his own of writing the Book of Mormon? And so on. It is apologetics: Jesus must have been the Son of God, since one would have expected him to be just one more peasant slob.

Again, Bultmann[1] figured it out: Mark must have found himself puzzled at the clash between the first section and a current proverb attributed to Jesus, which survives in its original form as saying 31 in the Gospel of Thomas: "No prophet is accepted in his own village; no physician heals those who know him." So he decided to stitch them together so that the proverb would reinterpret the original story. Really it *reverses* the meaning of verses 1–3a. Now we are to believe the synagogue audience was *affronted* at Jesus' wisdom and healings! As if these things meant Jesus, a small-town non-entity like them, is acting "uppity"! And as a result he does not heal any of them, because he *cannot*, prevented by their lack of faith, which Mark says amazed Jesus. But actually what is hindering him is that darn proverb! What a mess!

Matthew could not resist tinkering. He did nothing to smooth out the sudden about-face of the crowd, but he felt uneasy with the notion that Jesus *could* not heal these little-faiths, as well as the idea that Jesus was surprised at their skepticism. So he

---

[1] Bultmann, *History of the Synoptic Tradition*, p. 31.

changes both. In Matthew's retelling, Jesus simply *did* not heal anybody who had anything worse than a case of the sniffles. ("Lord, I am affected by a bald patch!")[2] Why? What is the *matter*, Matt? Matthew seems to have a higher Christology than Mark did. Remember how Mark apparently saw nothing amiss in Jesus lining up for a baptism for the remission of sins, but Matthew downplayed it. Matthew could not imagine the divine Savior ("God with us") repenting of sins, which he could not possibly have committed. This time Matthew finds it unpalatable for the divine Jesus to be limited by any outward factor—or being surprised at anything! Must he not have been omniscient? And omnipotent? He must have been *punishing* those townspeople! They were *unworthy* of being healed!

Luke rewrites the synagogue rejection scene pretty drastically. He locates it in Nazareth (Luke 4:16), though Mark and Matthew do not specify the name of "his own country" (Mark 6:1; Matt. 13:54). Mark, followed by Matthew, has Jesus preach in the local synagogue but gives no idea what he was preaching about. The custom was that a visiting guest might be invited to comment on the text appointed for the day (Acts 13:14–15), so our gospel writers probably assumed that is what Jesus was doing. But Luke explicitly says Jesus was handed the scroll containing Isaiah. The trouble is that Luke's chosen passage is not a single text but two combined, Isaiah 61:1–2a and 58:6. Thus it is the product Luke's own composition. Jesus announces that he is there today to fulfill this passage(s), by which he apparently means he is ready to perform whatever healings these people may need. But Luke makes the car swerve off the road. He has Jesus antagonize his hearers: "I know what you are thinking! I have healed people in Capernaum, so why not here? But remember Elijah and Elisha did their miracles, not for fellow Israelites, but for pagans!"[3] Here we see an arbitrary reversal just as we did in Mark's version. Mark did not tell us what could have turned the congregation against Jesus, so Luke thought he ought to supply it. In the same way, remember,

---

[2] Graham Chapman, John Cleese, Terry Gilliam, Eric Idle, Terry Jones, and Michael Palin, *Monty Python's Life of Brian (of Nazareth)* (New York: Ace Books, 1979), p. 109.

[3] My paraphrase, obviously.

Luke thought the Markan story of Peter's recruitment required a more spectacular motivation, so he added the fish miracle. But Luke has only made matters worse here in chapter 4! Why on earth would Jesus intentionally provoke a friendly hometown crowd to try to *lynch* him (Luke 4:29)? Luke seems to be jumping the gun, anticipating those scenes in Acts where Paul has had it with Jewish opposition and announces he will henceforth preach only to Gentiles (Acts 13:45–46; 18:6; 28:23).

John has retained a couple of elements from Luke's version, only he sets them amid Jesus' visits to Jerusalem:

About the middle of the feast Jesus went up into the temple and taught. The Jews marveled at it, saying, "How is it that this man has learning, when he has never studied?" So Jesus answered them, "My teaching is not mine, but his who sent me…" Some of the people of Jerusalem therefore said, "Is not this the man whom they seek to kill? And here he is, speaking openly, and they say nothing to him! Can it be that the authorities really know that this is the Christ? Yet we know where this man comes from; and when the Christ appears, no one will know where he comes from." So Jesus proclaimed, as he taught in the temple, "You know me, and you know where I come from. But I have not come of my own accord; he who sent me is true, and him you do not know. I know him, for I come from him, and he sent me." So they sought to arrest him; but no one laid hands on him, because his hour had not yet come. Yet many of the people believed in him; they said, "When the Christ appears, will he do more signs than this man has done?" (John 7:14–16, 25–31).

Here Jesus is teaching, albeit in the Jerusalem temple, not in the Galilean synagogue. The hearers are amazed at his wisdom as one without scribal training, as in Mark. But his undistinguished Galilean origins are a stumbling block for some: should not Messiah just appear out of nowhere? And, a la Luke, he fires off an insult: they are ignorant of God. So finally, as in Luke, they try to apprehend him, but (again, as in Luke) he manages to make a supernaturally easy escape. And again there is awed mention of his reported miracles.

You see? These differences cannot be harmonized. They *are* inconsistencies, but they are not mistakes or goofs. They are editorial rewrites.

Repentance by Itself

Jesus appeared in Galilee preaching that, since the kingdom of God was imminent, people must repent, stop sinning, because soon the axe will fall. All those who do not produce a harvest of good deeds and good character will face the judgmental fires of Gehenna. There is still time, but just barely. Given this, to envision Jesus trying to form a new, ongoing community, whether a Church, a new religion, or a reformed Israelite commonwealth—is just absurd. There is room for all sorts of theories about what Jesus saw as his mission; I am not talking about this. Rather, I am pursuing the issue of clashing representations of Jesus' teachings in the gospels. These differences are not surprising once we recognize that the gospels are not simply records of what the historical Jesus said and did. They are mighty trees with many rings, layer upon layer of beliefs held by the successive redactors and the various communities for whom they wrote. This, for example, makes nonsense of the oftheard claim that, since in the New Testament only Jesus referred to himself as the Son of Man, the nomenclature must go back to Jesus himself. Who do such scholars think wrote the gospels? Jesus? When a Christian gospel writer depicts Jesus calling himself the Son of Man, we have a Christian other than Jesus calling Jesus the Son of Man, do we not? And the same holds true of *any* gospel teachings: a historical Jesus *may* have taught so-and-so, but we can be *sure* Christians taught it in Jesus' name. That is true in any case, is it not? In this section, the big question will be whether Jesus preached repentance as the means of salvation, much as John the Baptist before him had, or whether he preached the need to believe in him as the criterion of salvation.

Many scholars would, very reasonably, plot it out like this: the Proclaimer became the Proclaimed.[4] The medium turned into the message, the messenger became the Messiah. The turning point would have been the death and resurrection of Jesus (whether you consider those as historical events or as myth and hallucination). I find that the proposed case is clearer when we consider a parallel with the Prophet Muhammad. During his prophetic ministry he preached the message of "God and the Last Day." But he died, and the Islamic creed became "There is no God but God, and Muhammad is the Apostle of God." The proclaimer became the proclaimed. In the transitional phase, the idea was that "Muhammad was right! And we are carrying on his mission/message!" (Obviously, if you thought Muhammad was a fake and a con man, you would have no further interest in his message.) But the emphasis began to shift, so that Muhammad became as important, in a sense, as God. Sound familiar? At first, for a Christian to say she believed in Jesus meant that she was heeding his demand for repentance, even though he himself was no longer present. But eventually Jesus becomes the very heart of the gospel message. There were attempts to keep things in perspective, such having "Jesus" say, "Whoever believes in me, believes *not* in me, but in him who sent me" (John 12:44). But you know what finally happened: "Thomas replied, 'My Lord and my God!'" (John 20:28).

But the Christological evolution evident in the series of gospels from Mark to Matthew to John 12:44 to John 20:28) does not mean that each gospel embodies a successive ring of the Christological tree. No, I think it is more likely that the gospels are more or less simultaneous and co-existent. All the gospels' Christologies and salvation messages represent early Christian pluralism of a sort. In short, I think Mark did believe that, as Jesus said, one need "only" repent to be saved. John, by contrast, believed that faith in Jesus as the Christ was the ticket. "You will die in your sins unless you believe that I am he" (John 8:24).

---

[4] Rudolf Bultmann, *Theology of the New Testament.* Trans. Kendrick Groebel. Scribners Studies in Contemporary Theology (New York: Scribners, 1951), p. 33.

Before Bultmann, Adolf Harnack pointed out the same incongruity, saying that it cannot be that Jesus told the parable of the Prodigal Son, guaranteeing salvation for simple repentance, if he knew that, only a few weeks hence, that plan of salvation would be outmoded in favor of a new gospel of faith in Jesus and his cross.

> He takes the publican in the temple, the widow and her mite, the lost son, as his examples; none of them know anything about "Christology," and yet by his humility the publican was justified. These are facts that cannot be turned and twisted without doing violence to the grandeur and simplicity of Jesus' message in one of its most important aspects. To contend that Jesus meant his whole message to be taken provisionally, and everything in it to receive a different interpretation after his death and resurrection, nay, parts of it to be put aside as of no account, is a desperate supposition.[5]

Harnack took this inconsistency as proof that the religion *of* Jesus (the one he preached) had been replaced (actually corrupted) by the religion *about* Jesus. But I would see in the difference an example of the transitional stage. Luke does have Paul requiring faith in Jesus for salvation (16:31), but earlier he has Peter preach the need for repentance, then capped off by baptism in the miracle-working Name of Jesus (Acts 2:38; 4:10, 12). As earlier in Luke, the issue is repentance and forgiveness. Naturally, in the gospel narrative, it is Jesus himself who preaches this message, and he is not a part of it, just as Muhammad did not preach himself, but only "Allah and the Last Day." But in Acts, the sequel to Luke, Jesus is no longer around to preach his message, so Peter and Paul are left to repeat it, crediting it to Jesus: "Remember Jesus? He was right! Time to repent and be saved!" Throughout both Luke and Acts, salvation is not predicated upon Jesus' death as some kind of sacrificial atonement. Luke 22:27 omits this element from Mark

---

[5] Adolf Harnack, *What Is Christianity?* Trans. Thomas Bailey Saunders. (New York: Harper & Row, 1957), p. 143.

10:45, and Luke 22:20a cuts it likewise from Mark 14:24.[6] The only apparent exception, Acts 20:28, is textually uncertain and may be an interpolation.

INRI and IRS

How did Jesus feel about tax collectors? Did he feel like the rest of us? Or did he enjoy their company? Mark 2:15–17 says he sought them out:

> And as he sat at table in his house, many tax collectors and sinners were sitting with Jesus and his disciples; for there were many who followed him. And the scribes of the Pharisees, when they saw that he was eating with sinners and tax collectors, said to his disciples, "Why does he eat with tax collectors and sinners?" And when Jesus heard it, he said to them, "Those who are well have no need of a physician, but those who are sick; I came not to call the righteous, but sinners."

But Matthew 18:15–17 implies that, like most of us, he avoided them like the plague!

> If your brother sins against you, go and tell him his fault, between you and him alone. If he listens to you, you have gained your brother. But if he does not listen, take one or two others along with you, that every word may be confirmed by the evidence of two or three witnesses. If he refuses to listen to them, tell it to the church; and if he refuses to listen even to the church, let him be to you as a Gentile and a tax collector.

Why this seemingly drastic difference? It is a genuine contradiction, for sure. But why? Had Jesus been surprised by a whopping tax bill between the two incidents? Probably not. The Mark passage depicts Jesus as following the (apocryphal) example

---

[6] Luke 22:19b–20 appears to be a later addition to the text in order to harmonize Luke with Mark.

of Moses' brother Aaron. He used to address notorious sinners with a friendly greeting, which surprised them but also gratified them. Thereafter, when the crook is planning some new misadventure, he stops and thinks, "If I do this, how can I face Aaron next time I see him?" And, likely as not, he nixes the scheme and goes look for honest work.[7] The punch line tells it all. Jesus seeks out sinners in order to persuade them to repent, to assure them no one is beyond the pale of God's forgiveness. So should he restrict himself to the fellowship of the already-repentant? Does that not kind of defeat the purpose?

On the other hand, the scribes' objection was not completely unreasonable either. As it says in 1 Corinthians 15:33, quoting the playwright Menander, "Bad company corrupts good character." But Mark's Jesus must have figured it works both ways.

It is also possible, as Louise Schottroff suggests,[8] that the "publicans" or toll collectors, like Luke's Zachaeus, got a bad rap and were not necessarily Roman stooges and traitors exploiting their own people. If this is true, then they were one more group of despised outcasts like lepers and demoniacs to whom Jesus reached out.

But then how to account for Matthew's Jesus commanding his community to shun the excommunicated—as if they were loathsome tax collectors? The word "community" gives us the clue. Jesus is made to stipulate rules for discipline in a sectarian group ("the church," verse 17) like the Qumran Essenes, who also practiced the shunning of reprobates. That is the explicit setting for the same arrangements obtaining in the Pauline church at Corinth (1 Cor. 5:1–5). But does that describe the wandering troupe of St. Francis-style mendicants led by Jesus? No. It is anachronistic here. Someone is trying to hang such disciplinary rules on Jesus to claim his authority, and whoever it was had forgotten how Jesus had reached out to the tax men instead of shunning them.

---

[7] Solomon Schechter, *Some Aspects of Rabbinic Theology* (New York: Macmillan, 1910), p. 321.

[8] Louise Schottroff, "Tax Collectors." In Louise Schottroff and Wolfgang Stegemann, *Jesus of Nazareth the Hope of the Poor*. Trans. Matthew J. O'Connell (Maryknoll: Orbis Books, 1986), pp. 7–13.

Fast Times at Nazareth High

This one is complicated, since we find *three* distinct positions on the practice of fasting attributed to Jesus. Unless perhaps he suffered from Multiple Personality Syndrome, it seems unlikely that all of the opinions actually go back to a historical Jesus! Mark 2:18–23 splices two of them together:[9]

> Now John's disciples and the Pharisees were fasting; and people came and said to him, "Why do John's disciples and the disciples of the Pharisees fast, but your disciples do not fast?" And Jesus said to them, *"Can the wedding guests fast while the bridegroom is with them? As long as they have the bridegroom with them, they cannot fast. The days will come, when the bridegroom is taken away from them, and then they will fast in that day.* No one sews a piece of unshrunk cloth on an old garment; if he does, the patch tears away from it, the new from the old, and a worse tear is made. And no one puts new wine into old wineskins; if he does, the wine will burst the skins, and the wine is lost, and so are the skins; but new wine is for fresh skins."

The italicized material represents one opinion, equivalent to the well-known text from Ecclesiastes 3:1–9:

> For everything there is a season, and a time for every matter under heaven:
> a time to be born, and a time to die;
> a time to plant, and a time to pluck up what is planted;
> a time to kill, and a time to heal;
> a time to break down, and a time to build up;

---

[9] Why would Mark do this? He has done the same thing elsewhere; e.g. he has inserted the originally stand-alone story of the woman with the blood flow (5:24b–34) between the halves of that of Jairus' daughter (5:21–24a, 35–41). He interlaced the cursing of the fig tree (11:12–14, 20–21) with the cleansing of the temple (11:11, 15–19). He interrupted the visit of Jesus' relatives (3:19b–21, 31–35) with the Beelzebul Controversy (3:22–30). He wanted to have one story comment on the other.

a time to weep, and a time to laugh;
a time to mourn, and a time to dance;
a time to cast away stones, and a time to gather stones together;
a time to embrace, and a time to refrain from embracing;
a time to seek, and a time to lose;
a time to keep, and a time to cast away;
a time to rend, and a time to sew;
a time to keep silence, and a time to speak;
a time to love, and a time to hate;
a time for war, and a time for peace.

It *might* mean the same as this, but obviously the followers of the customs taught by the Pharisees and the Baptizer did not fast *all the time*. So *what* if Jesus' disciples kept to a different schedule of fasting? But then that is not what Jesus' critics' question suggests: Jesus' followers *no longer practice fasting at all*.

Another, more common reading is to make this part of the passage an (anachronistic) explanation that Jesus' followers will get back to fasting soon enough: after Jesus is arrested and executed, but for the present, they are rejoicing that he is with them. Some interpreters go so far as to suggest this is an etiology for the post-Jesus practice of fasting on Fridays, commemorating Good Friday, when Jesus was taken away. Remember Bultmann's observation: when the behavior of the disciples and *not of Jesus himself* is questioned, we are dealing with the practice of the (post-Jesus) Church.

The rest of the Markan text seems to mean that the kingdom of God has arrived (at least in some sense: cf, Matt. 12:28), and that, accordingly, fasting is now obsolete, given that it was a penitential exercise aimed at bringing (or preparing for) the advent of the kingdom. In other words, *fasting is over*. The Gospel of Thomas takes this latter position, but even more dramatically: "His disciples asked and said to him: 'Do you want us to fast? How shall we pray, how shall we give alms? What rules concerning eating shall we follow?'" (Saying 6, Jean Doresse translation). The original answer is to be found over in Saying 14: "Jesus says to them: 'When you fast, you will beget sin for yourselves; when you pray, you will be condemned; when you give alms, you will do evil to your souls!'" Also, see Saying 51: "His disciples said to him: 'On what day shall rest come to those who are dead, and on what day shall the new world come?' He said to them: 'This that you wait for has come, and you have not recognized it.'" Also Saying 113: "His disciples said to him: 'On what day will the kingdom come?' 'It will not come when it is expected. No one will say: "See, it is here!" or "Look, it is there!" but the Kingdom of the Father is spread over the earth and men do not see it.'"

It is reminiscent of Shankara (eighth century CE), the great theologian of Advaita (Non-dualist) Vedanta Hinduism: once one attains enlightenment, all conventional religious exercises, once quite appropriate, are rendered utterly pointless, childish things to be put away. To persist in them is to remain in the unredeemed state. Matthew 6:16–18 says,

> And when you fast, do not look dismal, like the hypocrites, for they disfigure their faces that their fasting may be seen by men. Truly, I say to you, they have received their reward. But when you fast, anoint your head and wash your face, that your fasting may not be seen by men but by your Father who is in secret; and your Father who sees in secret will reward you.

Fasting is back! Just do not make a show of it. Note that here it is simply taken for granted that Christians will fast. Why the difference from the previous passages? Here we are hearing the voice of Matthean Jewish Christianity, in competition with both the Formative Judaism of the Yavneh Rabbis and Pauline Christianity. We find a related sentiment in Luke 5:39, which the evangelist tacked onto the end of the wine-and-wineskins text he borrowed from Mark: "And no one after drinking old wine desires new; for he says, 'The old is good enough for me.'" Here is a prime example of a later writer "correcting" a text of which he does not approve but which he is not at liberty to omit altogether. The Markan original, in Luke's estimation, goes much too far. Luke is thinking of Marcion who believed true Christianity has nothing in common with Judaism and thus repudiated its observances. Luke scoffs at this, making Jesus point out that anyone with taste and sophistication prefers aged, fine wine, i.e. Jewish (or Jewish-derived) piety.

Again, it is futile and wrong-headed to try to disentangle these various threads as if they all had to come from Jesus and must be homogenized into a single, consistent position. If that is what you are doing, you have got the Bible all wrong. You are muzzling it, not elucidating it.

The Rich Young Rules

Mark apparently found nothing amiss in the inquirer's question for Jesus: "Good Teacher, what must I do to inherit eternal life?" (Mark 10:17), or with Jesus' initial response: Wait just a second there! "Why do you call me 'good'? No one is good except for God himself!" (Mark 10:18). The same cannot be said for Matthew. He will not have Jesus disclaiming his (absolute) goodness! As if Jesus' self-effacing modesty is not itself a mark of his goodness! Jesus, recoiling from the danger of mere flesh boasting before God Almighty (Eph. 2:9; 1 Cor. 1:29), will not accept the praise. You might say the Rich Young Ruler is, like Peter in Mark 8:31–33, unwittingly functioning as a mouthpiece of Satan, naively unaware that his well-intended words constitute a temptation for Jesus. That is how it looks to me at any rate. As such, these verses should not have given Matthew a Christological migraine. It has no ontological implications. But it did make his temples pound. So Matthew changed the wording. First, in his retelling, the inquirer now asks, "Teacher, what *good deed* must I do to have eternal life?" (Matt. 19:16). Jesus, then, is no longer on the hot seat. And his answer is different, too: "Why do you *ask me about what is good*? One there is who is good" (Matt. 19:17). Or is that the best translation? I am convinced by O. Lamar Cope,[10] who argues that it should be rendered "The good is one," referring to the unity of the Torah. That is, one cannot choose one of the commandments and make it the criterion for salvation. The point is

---

[10] O. Lamar Cope, *Matthew: A Scribe Trained for the Kingdom of Heaven.* Catholic Biblical Quarterly (Washington D.C.: Catholic Biblical Association, 1976), "The Good Is One" – Mt 19:16–22 and Prov 3:35–4:4," pp. 111–120.

similar to that made in James 2:10–11: "For whoever keeps the whole law but fails in one point has become guilty of all of it. For he who said, 'Do not commit adultery,' said also, 'Do not kill.' If you manage not to commit adultery but do kill, you have nonetheless become a transgressor of the law."

Another change is perhaps more subtle, but, I think, quite significant nonetheless. In Mark Jesus lists several biblical commandments, and the man unselfconsciously replies that, of course he knows them and in fact has kept them since childhood—but what *else*? Jesus sees the fellow is ready for more, so in Mark he replies, "You lack one thing. Sell your possessions, give to the poor, and you will have treasure in heaven, and come, follow me" (Mark 10:21). Matthew has the man say, "What do I still lack?" So it is no longer Jesus who mentions a "lack," but the inquirer. And now Jesus prefaces his reply instead with "If you would be perfect..." What's the difference, you ask? Matthew writes at a later institutional stage, when stringent requirements for all Christians have been somewhat relaxed, so that only the elite, the most committed, are to follow them.[11] This is why Roman Catholics call the Matthean version "councils of perfection" applicable only to monks, nuns, and priests, not the laity.

Why did Matthew feel inclined to make *both* of these alterations? Are they somehow linked? Indeed they are. On the one hand, he does not want Jesus to be caught disclaiming the prerogative of deity, absolute goodness. On the other, he seems to reserve the voluntary poverty requirement to the "perfect," letting the conventionally pious off the hook. Protestant philosopher Max Scheler provides the link (though he is not treating this passage in particular). He theorizes that in the evolution of any religion (e.g. Christianity, Buddhism), when the founder is eventually deified by his followers, his divinity is believed to have made possible his ability to live out the radical ethical demands he issues (cf, the Sermon on the Mount). No mortal, or very few, it is reasoned, could possibly live up to that standard. And if it takes a god to do it, it would be sheer effrontery for mere mortal slobs like you and

---

[11] Max Scheler, *Problems of a Sociology of Knowledge.* Trans. Manfred S. Frings (London: Routledge & Kegan Paul, 1980), pp. 84–85.

me to imagine *we* might do these things! So two conclusions follow. Only the radical few may or should dare to imitate the divine founder. And the superhuman Savior has fulfilled his discipleship demands *for* us! Thus Matthew's Jesus has become divine, which is why he has no need of John's baptism of repentance and why he *does* not, rather than *cannot*, heal unbelievers at Nazareth. This is why Matthew 23:34 attributes directly to Jesus words that, in Luke 11:49, are ascribed instead to Divine Wisdom.[12]

There is yet another version of the Rich Young Ruler story, found in John chapter three. This is so thorough a re-write of Mark that I hesitate to call the differences between the accounts "contradictions." But, again, it may prove enriching to explain some of the changes. First, though the Synoptic versions (Matt. 19:16–22; Mark 10:17–22; Luke 18:18–23) give the seeker no name, John names him "Nicodemus," which means "ruler of the people." And Luke 18:18 calls him "a ruler," though Matthew and Mark have simply "a man." This would be one of the very many places where Luke and John agree with each other while differing from Matthew and Mark.[13] I think John read Luke, at least in some edition. And this explains a couple of things.

First, why does the Johannine Jesus suddenly broach the question of how to be saved, when Nicodemus has conspicuously not asked it? Because he *does* ask it in Luke 18:18 (as in Matthew and Mark, of course). John takes the question for granted, then

---

[12] M. Jack Suggs, *Wisdom, Christology, and Law in Matthew's Gospel* (Cambridge: Harvard University Press, 1970), pp. 58–61. "His alterations in chapter 11 show that, for him, Sophia is *identified* with Jesus. Jesus is Sophia incarnate" (p. 58).

[13] Pierson Parker ("Luke and the Fourth Evangelist") explains the parallels as the result of Luke and John ("John Mark," as in Acts 12:12) working together in evangelistic ministry. C.H. Dodd, Frederick Grant, and John Amedee Bailey (*The Traditions Common to the Gospels of Luke and John*) chalk it all up to fortuitous use of common oral traditions. F. Lamar Cribbs (*A Study of the Contacts That Exist Between St. Luke and St. John*) argues for Luke's use of John or of the pre-Johannine Signs Gospel. Note that wherever Luke has a parallel to Matthew/Mark, he follows it, but where there is a Johannine version as well as a Matthean/Markan version, Luke skips Matthew/Mark and parallels John instead (or opts for a version like none of the other evangelists).

supplies a rather, but not completely, different answer. "Truly, truly, I say unto you, unless one is *born anew*, he cannot see the kingdom of God" (John 3:3). So far, we have a close parallel to Luke 18:17, the verse immediately preceding the introduction of the ruler: "Truly, I say to you, whoever does not receive the kingdom of God *like a child* shall *not enter it*." But John's Jesus does not go on to cite Torah commandments or to suggest voluntary poverty. We saw how Matthew "updated" Jesus' answer, restricting these stringent requirements to an elite. John, too, adjusts Jesus' requirement: "Truly, truly, I say unto you, unless one is born of water and the Spirit, he *cannot enter* the kingdom of God" (3:5). Now one must be baptized.[14]

John's Nicodemus character appears to stand for Jewish elders who embraced Christianity but dared not publicly say so lest they be excommunicated from the synagogue (cf, John 9:22).[15] John implies that such Jewish crypto-Christians are, by their fearful silence, already denying him before men (Mark 8:38) and so cannot be saved. "Stand up, stand up for Jesus!"

Finally, we must note that the phrase "the kingdom of God" is as rare in the Gospel of John as it is abundant in the Synoptics (though Matthew does generally change it to "kingdom of heaven"). In fact the two instances of it here in John chapter 3 are the only times it appears in John, which points decisively to John's use of Synoptic material.

Did Jesus Permit Divorce?

Jesus is asked for his opinion on a matter much discussed in first-century Judaism, namely allowable justifications for divorcing a man's wife. The discussions were occasioned by the (intentional?) vagueness of Deuteronomy 24:1–4:

---

[14] Pardon me if I do not take seriously the pathetic attempts of non-sacramentalists to make this verse mean something else. Ironically, the so-called Baptists are the chief of sinners when it comes to this. Among Evangelical Protestants, only the Campbellites are honest with it.

[15] Raymond E. Brown, *The Community of the Beloved Disciple: The Life, Loves, and Hates of an Individual Church in New Testament Times* (New York: Paulist Press, 1979), pp. 71–73.

> When a man takes a wife and marries her, if then she finds no favor in his eyes because he has found *some indecency* in her, and he writes her a bill of divorce and puts it in her hand and sends her out of his house, and she departs out of his house, and if she goes and becomes another man's wife, and the latter husband dislikes her and writes her a bill of divorce and puts it in her hand and sends her out of his house, or if the latter husband dies, who took her to be his wife, then her former husband, who sent her away, may not take her again to be his wife, after she has been defiled; for that is an abomination before [Jehovah], and you shall not bring guilt upon the land which [Jehovah] your God gives you for an inheritance.

"Some indecency"? What's *that* supposed to mean? As Elaine Benes would say, "It means whatever the hell you *want* it to mean!" And that is why liberal Pharisee Hillel (110 BCE – 10 CE) taught that a man could divorce his wife for burning his dinner (an intentionally trivial example)! But his very strict colleague and rival sage Shammai (50 BCE – 30 CE) decided that "Moses" must have meant to allow divorce only if the wife were proven an adulteress. That would qualify as "indecency," for sure, but is that *all* it might mean? Hoo boy…

So when some Pharisees asked Jesus to weigh in on the matter, it need not have been some kind of trick "gotcha" question such as his opponents often fired at him, like hostile moderators at presidential debates.[16] Mark 10:2–12:

> And Pharisees came up and in order to test him asked, "Is it lawful for a man to divorce his wife?" He answered them, "What did Moses command you?" They said, "Moses allowed a man to write a certificate of divorce, and to put her away." But Jesus said to them, "For your hardness of heart he wrote you this commandment. But from the beginning of

---

[16] I know it says they asked him this question in order to "test" him, but this time I get the impression it means they wanted to *assess* him: where does he stand on the issue?

creation, 'God made them male and female.' 'For this reason a man shall leave his father and mother and be joined to his wife,[a] and the two shall become one flesh.' So they are no longer two but one flesh. What therefore God has joined together, let not man put asunder." And in the house the disciples asked him again about this matter. And he said to them, "Whoever divorces his wife and marries another, commits adultery against her; and if she divorces her husband and marries another, she commits adultery."

Luke 16:18 parallels Mark 10:12, but the rest is lacking. Matthew 5:31–32 and 19: 3–9 largely agree with Mark, with one key exception. Matthew adds "except for *porneia*," whatever that means. It is evident that Matthew has decided to restore the strategic ambiguity of Deuteronomy, to allow greater flexibility for Christians in his community who had found themselves in incompatible marriages that did not involve adultery but had become intolerable nonetheless. If he had meant adultery only, he could have used the Greek word *moicheia*. The word *porneia* has a broader range of meaning, originally denoting "prostitution," though it seems that the only kind of prostitution condemned in the Old Testament was that of a married woman turning tricks on the side to make a little extra cookie jar money as in Proverbs chapter 7). It is conceivable this is in view in Matthew's use of the word here, but it is also possible it refers to marriage outside the usual Jewish lines, e.g., to a cousin or to a Gentile. Some think this is what is forbidden to Gentile Christian converts in Acts 15:20 where *porneia* is rendered as "unchastity." I suspect that in 1 Corinthians 6:13, 18, given the context, it refers to Christians patronizing pagan temple prostitutes (precisely as in Revelation 2:14, 20). In view is the libertine (1 Cor. 6:12, "All things are lawful for me") Gnostics like the Nicolaitans (expressly named in Revelation 2:15). But we do not know for sure, and I am guessing that is no accident.

Is Matthew fibbing here, trying to get us to believe Jesus said something that in fact he did not say? Of course not! Do you not see what is going on here? The whole Gospel of Matthew is a manual to guide Jewish Christian missionaries to the nations, those readers who wear the mask of the disciples receiving the Great Commission at Matthew 28:18–20. It is, in effect, a kind of Constitution to govern Christian behavior in the new churches to be founded. And the addition of "except for *porneia*" is an amendment to that quasi-legal text, not an attempt to falsify the teaching of Jesus. Think of it as akin to what Moses does when approached by the daughters of the late Zelophehad in Numbers 27:7. There was no male heir; why should the daughters not inherit? God told Moses to amend the Constitution: "The daughters of Zelophehad are right; you shall give them possession of an inheritance among their father's brethren and cause the inheritance of their father to pass to them." Again, it is like the scribe who added "without cause" to Matthew 5:22. It was just too severe—better mitigate it!

Matthew, I say, certainly viewed Jesus as a latter-day Moses, issuing a new Torah full of commandments. But Martin Dibelius, one of the pioneer form critics, wondered if in every case Jesus originally intended his maxims to have legal force.[17] Jesus admits that Mosaic law provides for divorce because we are mere human beings, not perfect angels, and what good is a law that assumes we can live like angels? It is a tragic shame that we have hard hearts, but we do, and some accommodation must be made. God designed marriage to be insoluble; that is his perfect will. But what are you going to do? So if Jesus says "What God has joined together, let no mere mortal divide asunder," is he laying down the law? It is an imperative, but is it more of a statement of the ideal for which you should strive? Maybe you ought to think twice before kicking your wife out for ruining your steak.

Forever Family Values

Did Jesus teach about appropriate family values? I am afraid it is the wrong question. Jesus is not exactly shown treating this as a distinct topic. Instead, there are a few passages that touch only tangentially upon parents and filial responsibilities. For instance,

---

[17] Martin Dibelius, *The Message of Jesus Christ: The Tradition of the Earliest Christian Communities.* Trans. Frederick C. Grant. (New York: Scribners, 1939), pp. 152–153.

Jesus takes for granted that parents, with all their flaws, would never think of denying reasonable requests from their children (Matt. 7:9–11). But that is almost beside the point; he is really teaching about the Heavenly Father and confidence in prayer.

Mark chapter 7 embroils Jesus in a dispute with scribes, initially about ritual purity, but finally about the tradition of the elders, the Oral Torah. Jesus takes the example of the Corban rule whereby a faithful Jew could yank the rug out from under his aging parents and pledge their support money to the temple treasury instead. Have they somehow forgotten the commandment "You shall honor your father and mother"? What an irony! Oral extrapolation from the scripture has not extended the meaning of the sacred text, as claimed, but *nullified* it! Jesus of course takes for granted that we ought to honor our parents and tend to them in their old age, but technically his point is not to reiterate the commandment. It is rather a *Tu Quo Que* argument (actually a logical fallacy): your opponent is caught undermining his own position by contradicting it. "Your oral tradition is no good! Look at the results!"

Some anti-biblicists like to point to Luke 14:26 as proof that Jesus was an insane fanatic with the worst family values possible: "If any one comes to me and does not hate his own father and mother and wife and children and brothers and sisters, yes, and even his own life, he cannot be my disciple." This does sound pretty bad on first reading, but I understand it as a martyrdom saying. It describes the sort of situation, e.g., of the second-century noblewoman Perpetua, arrested for her faith and condemned to arena. Her family brought Perpetua's newborn infant to her cell and pleaded with her to renounce her illegal creed for the sake of her baby. But she was steadfast in her refusal. I think this is what Jesus' saying means. "Hate" in such a context means "despise, disdain," as in Hebrews 12:2 which says that Jesus himself went to the cross "despising the shame." Likewise John 12:25: "He who loves his life loses it, and he who hates his life in this world will keep it for eternal life." In other words, he who counts this life as worthless in comparison to the next (Phil. 3:8: "Indeed I count everything as loss because of the surpassing worth of knowing Christ Jesus my Lord. For his sake I have suffered the loss of all things, and count them as refuse, in order that I may gain Christ"). Actually, it seems to me that Matthew 10:37 ("He who loves father or mother more than me is not worthy of me; and he who loves son or daughter more than me is not worthy of me") gets it right. Persecutors are forcing Christians into "Sophie's choice."

Jesus is not being very respectful to his mother at the Cana wedding when she suggests he employ his magic to restock the wine (John 2:4). But this is not really biographical material. As Raymond E. Brown[18] demonstrates, this anecdote must come from the stream of Infancy Gospel fiction such as we read in the Infancy Gospel of Thomas. There young Jesus, already possessing more-than-human intelligence, saves the day when the stupid adults around him show their incompetence. Joseph, a bumbling carpenter, cannot seem to get all four chair legs the same length, but Jesus makes them uniform with a touch. Jesus goes to a private tutor but shows he knows more than the instructor, etc. Jesus is arrogant and bratty in all of them, as he is here. John has merely added the disciples to the scene and made Jesus older.

Similarly, Mark 3:20–21, 31–35 constitute neither any general teaching on family nor genuine biographical data. Instead, it is a piece of early church factional polemic. One faction of Jewish Christians venerated the Holy Family, or the Pillars (Gal. 2:9), as their figureheads. Another revered the Twelve as their authorities. The situation precisely paralleled that of the Sunni sect and the Shi'a sect of early Islam. The former held to the teachings of the Companions of the Prophet Muhammad, while the latter looked to the Pillars, the blood relatives of the Prophet. The scene in Mark chapter 3 advances the claims of the Twelve (and their successors, which is really the point), while having Jesus rebuff his family and their presumption of priority. Exactly like Galatians 2:6–9:

And from those who were reputed to be something (what they were makes no difference to me; God shows no partiality)— those, I say, who were of repute added nothing to me;

---

¹⁸ Brown, *Birth of the Messiah*, pp. 487–488.

…and…James and Cephas and John…were reputed to be pillars….

So these texts are not concerned with providing either teaching or examples of proper treatment of parents. The closest we come to the latter is John's crucifixion scene in which Jesus tells the Beloved Disciple to take care of his bereaved mother (John 19:26–27), though even here sectarian factionalism casts it shadow: otherwise, why not commit his mother to the care of his brothers?

Finally, there is the shocking Q passage Matthew 8:21–22 (cf, Luke 9:59–60): "Another of the disciples said to him, 'Lord, let me first go and bury my father.' But Jesus said to him, 'Follow me, and leave the dead to bury their own dead.'" Ouch! One of the most important acts of charity in Judaism was the burial of the dead who had no family or were despised criminals. This is why Joseph of Arimathea buried Jesus, after all. And see the Book of Tobit. But to *neglect the burial of one's own father*? That's a tough one. What is worse: this or "Corbanning" your parents' retirement?

But there *is* a likely explanation: the Synoptic gospels depict Jesus as announcing the soon-coming end of the world, in the light of which ordinary mundane factors were suspended. No time remains for niceties like burial rites or workaday jobs.[19] Job number one is to preach the news of the coming Judgment so people will be scared into repenting before the axe falls! In short, why take the trouble to bury old dad when he will be rising up again to face the music in no time? This is, admittedly, a cure worse than the disease! Okay, Jesus did not scoff at respectful treatment of parents—but that was because he was a deluded fanatic who imagined such customs had become moot! Take your pick.

---

[19] When speaking of the 1970s Children of God sect, Daniel Cohen describes their stance: "They often shock people, and they mean to. The hour is too late, they say, to stand on false dignity." Cohen, *The New Believers: Young Religion in America* (New York: Ballantine Books, 1975), p. 2.

No Man Knows the Day and the Hour
or the Century or the Millennium

Whether a historical Jesus predicted it or not, the early Christians avidly expected Jesus' Parousia ("presence, advent") at any time. But as time went by, the Christians dealt with their cognitive dissonance[20] with several rationalizations of the delay, mostly fabricated sayings of Jesus anticipating it, as little sense as it made to set a time *and to predict an unanticipated delay!* But anything starts looking pretty good when you are desperate. In historical retrospect, it is amazing to see how readily we disdainfully write off failed apocalyptic "prophets" like the Millerites, Jehovah's Witnesses, and Harold Camping and yet continue to wrestle with and reinterpret the very same embarrassing blunder that lies at the root of the Christian religion.

So Mark's gospel begins with Jesus announcing that the prophesied kingdom of God was about to dawn, and urging his contemporaries to clean up their act while there was still time. If this means anything at all, it means that the Great Denouement is hurtling on its way. There would be no way to make room for, e.g., the establishment of a new religious institution, or to conduct a worldwide evangelistic effort, though we now find verses suggesting such things and attributing them to Jesus.[21]

Mark 13 has Jesus providing an apocalyptic checklist to an inner circle of his disciples, a standard technique of later Gnostic treatises which used it to rationalize the novelty of their teachings: why had no one heard of these new "revelations" till now? The world wasn't ready to hear them yet, so Jesus entrusted these secrets to a select group to keep them in trust. *That*'s the ticket, sure! At any rate, by the end of the discourse, "Jesus" sets a deadline: "Truly I tell you, this generation shall not pass away till all these things have transpired" (Mark 13:30). That is readily tested if you wait long enough to see what happens – and nothing

---

[20] Leon Festinger, Henry W. Riecken, and Stanley Schachter, *When Prophecy Fails: A Social and Psychological Study of a Modern Group that Predicted the Destruction of the World.* (New York: Harper & Row, 1964).

[21] Werner Georg Kümmel, *Promise and Fulfilment: The Eschatology of Jesus.* Trans. Dorothea M. Barton. (London: SCM Press, 1961).

did. So there were several attempts to "correct" the Little Apocalypse, as it is called. In verses 7 and 8, someone is already hitting the breaks: the emergence of false messiahs, then the outbreak of wars and earthquakes—but "the end is not yet." And verse 10 shoehorns a world mission into the eschatological sequence. But the Parousia of Daniel's Son of Man will follow these events as surely and as quickly as summer follows on the heels of the blossoming of figs (verses 29–30). And you can bet heaven and earth on it (verse 30). That is a guarantee you can depend on!

Only you cannot. Jesus then backs up: "But of that day or that hour no one knows, not even the angels in heaven, nor the Son, but only the Father" (verse 32). Paul Wilhelm Schmiedel[22] swore that, if the historical Jesus ever said anything, he *must* have said *this*. Here is what would later be called the Criterion of Embarrassment: who could possibly have wanted to make Jesus admit he was ignorant about something? But the answer is simple! Someone who figured it would be better than having Jesus make a false prophecy!

Still another attempted rescue of the date-setting in Mark 13:30 occurs in Mark 9:1, "Truly, I say to you, there are some standing here who will not taste death before they see that the kingdom of God has come with power." In 13:30, it was the entire Jesus-generation that would behold the Tribulation and the Parousia. Now it is only "*some* standing here" who have that privilege. That has to mean that the saying comes from a time when by far most of that "greatest generation" had expired. But the redactional placement of the 9:1 saying in its present position attests an even later date, since it serves to reinterpret what the Parousia was supposed to be. Now we are to understand the advent of the Son of Man as the Transfiguration.[23] This is still a popular dodge today, blatantly silly as it is.

---

22 Paul Wilhelm Schmiedel, "Gospels," in T.K. Cheyne and J. Sutherland Black, eds., *Encyclopaedia: A Critical Dictionary of the Literary, Political and History, the Archæology, Geography and Natural History of the Bible* (London: Adam and Charles Black, 1914)

23 Second Peter 1:16–8 likewise redefines the "coming" of Jesus as the Transfiguration.

The Johannine Appendix (John 21) gives us the next step in the rationalization process: Jesus was "incorrectly" supposed to have predicted that at least the Beloved Disciple would endure to the end (the reference, of course, is to Mark 9:1), implying that he was the last known survivor—but he, too, died and nothing happened! But, oh, wait a minute: maybe we misinterpreted his words! Maybe all he meant was "If I were to decide he is to tarry till I come again, what business is it of yours, Pete?" Yeah! He didn't say it would actually *happen*; it was just hypothetical! Whew!

Second, Peter freely admits the "promised coming" of Christ failed to occur, but for a good reason! He has simply extended the original deadline in order to allow more time for stubborn unbelievers to repent and be saved. A single day? A millennium? It is all the same to God; he has got all the time in the world. And now, it seems, so do you!

The most drastic way of coming to terms with the failure of the Parousia was *demythologizing* the Eschaton. We find that, too, in the New Testament.[24] "The kingdom of God is not coming with signs to be observed, nor will they say, 'Lo! Here!' or 'There!' For the kingdom of God is within you" (Luke 17:20–21). "Truly, truly, I say to you, he who hears my word and believes him who sent me, has eternal life; he does not come into judgment, but *has passed* from death to life" (John 5:24). "Truly, truly, I say to you, the hour is coming, *and now is*, when the dead will hear the voice of the Son of God, and those who hear will live" (John 5:25). "Jesus said to her, 'Your brother will rise again.' Martha said to him, 'I know that he will rise again in the resurrection at the last day.' Jesus said to her, 'I am the resurrection and the life; he who believes in me, though he die, yet shall he live, and whoever lives and believes in me shall never die'" (John 11:24–26). "Judas (not Iscariot) said to him, 'Lord, how is it that you will manifest yourself to us, and not to the world?' Jesus answered him, 'If a man loves me, he will keep my word, and my Father will love him, and we will come to

---

[24] Rudolf Bultmann, *Jesus Christ and Mythology* (New York: Scribners, 1958), p. 32.

him and make our home with him'" (John 14:22–23). So much for "every eye shall see him"!

Even the much-vaunted notion of "inaugurated eschatology" or "eschatology in the process of realizing itself"[25] appears to be a salvage operation by the gospel writers, inserting bits of realized eschatology into stories that originally assumed straightforward futuristic eschatology, e.g. Matthew 12:28, where the Q version shared with Luke says Jesus' exorcisms prove the kingdom of God has arrived.[26] The story reads just fine without it, and Mark's version does not have it (Mark 3:22–30).

Could Jesus Keep a (Messianic) Secret?

No attentive reader of Mark's gospel will have missed the oddity of Jesus performing great deeds, then warning the beneficiaries to keep their mouths shut about it (Mark 1:44; 5:43; 7:36; 8:26). When he casts out demons he tells them to stop yelling out his secret identity as the Son of God (Mark 1:25, 34; 3:11–12). When these feats elicit revelations about his Messianic status, he tells his hearers to keep these under their burnooses, too (Mark 8:30; 9:9). You can hardly fail to notice, but it is not so easy to explain them. But they *can* be explained, and William Wrede *did* explain them.

Wrede knew from passages like Romans 1:3–4; Acts 2:36, and 13:30–35 that many Christians believed that Jesus became the Christ and Son of God at his resurrection (especially if the Transfiguration was originally a resurrection appearance story). Others, however, believed Jesus had been made Son of God at his baptism. This latter version was a product of the delay of the Parousia. Wrede reasoned that, if you believed Jesus was inaugurated King Messiah at Easter, this meant you didn't see Jesus' earthly ministry as Messianic. His imminent return would be

---

[25] Joachim Jeremias, *The Parables of Jesus*. Trans. S.H. Hooke (New York: Scribners, 1972), p. 230; Jeremias, *Theology of the New Testament*. Trans. John Bowden (London: SCM Press, 1971), pp. 96–108; George Eldon Ladd, *The Presence of the Future: The Eschatology of Biblical Realism* (Grand Rapids: Eerdmans, 1974).

[26] Reginald H. Fuller, *Interpreting the Miracles* (London: SCM Press, 1963), pp. 29–37.

his second coming as Jesus, but his first as Messiah. But he never showed up! So Christians decided Jesus' first coming was already as Messiah. What was the role of the Messiah? Whatever Jesus had done: healing, exorcizing, teaching, suffering, dying, and rising. And that all started at the Jordan baptism. Thus Jesus must have been ordained Messiah on that occasion. Mark (or some predecessor) hit upon a way of reconciling the two opposing views. Here is how he did it. Suppose Jesus was the Christ as far back as his baptism, but he kept it a closely guarded secret till his resurrection. It would be altogether natural for people to infer that he had only *become* the Christ at that point if this was the first time they'd heard of it. Mark was in effect saying, "You are *both* right—sort of," a gentle and friendly correction.

But his story of Jesus included episodes originally told from both of the perspectives. Okay, if he was going around doing Messianic deeds the whole time, how did people remain unaware of his Messianic identity? He… uh, must have told those who did know his true identity (or the deeds that should have suggested it) to keep it secret. The question remains, though: what was the point in terms of *narrative motivation?* Odysseus hid his identity so he could pursue his strategies undiscovered and unprevented. But Jesus' Messianic secrecy makes sense only *outside the narrative*, as an elaborate harmonization gimmick.

Matthew, Luke, and John are inconsistent: sometimes they use Mark's material containing the secrecy motifs, but sometimes they ignore it. For instance it is only Mark's Triumphal Entry story in which the crowd welcomes Jesus but without hailing him as the Messianic king, whereas all three of the others, albeit in slightly different words, have the crowd acclaiming him as Messiah. But what is still baffling is whether and why *Mark* seems occasionally to blab his Messiahship in public! He seems to pull rank, appealing to Messianic privilege or prerogative—or does he? Mostly it turns on the meaning of his use of the phrase "the Son of Man." Is it a synonym for "Messiah"? Many or most scholars think it is, but not all.

There are other non-Messianic uses and meanings.[27] Often the original Aramaic term *bar-nasha* (Hebrew: *bar-enosh*) simply meant "a man," referring to the common lot of men as exemplified in some individual under discussion, usually the speaker himself. "A man's gotta keep warm!" Which is why Macy's Thanksgiving parade Santa is drunk up on his float! Or "You really know how to hurt a guy," namely *me*.

Similarly, "son of man" was sometimes a self-reference in the context of impending or feared misfortune: "I guess a man has to go when his time comes!" "A man gets only so many chances!" It is sort of like trying to hide behind humanity in general so the Grim Reaper might not spot you in the crowd!

A brief overview of these "Son of Man" passages seems in order. First, several texts make good sense as ordinary self-references, though the Greek-speaking authors of the gospels may no longer have realized that. When Jesus defends his allowing his men to glean wheat on Saturday, he says, "The Sabbath was made for man, not man for the Sabbath; wherefore the son of man is master of the Sabbath" (Mark 2:27–28), echoing a famous rabbinical saying, "The Sabbath is delivered unto you; you are not delivered unto it." The point is not his or anybody's Messianic authority, but rather the humanitarian intent of the Sabbath.

He says to the paralyzed man, "Your sins are forgiven," appealing to God's delegation of healing and forgiving authority to mortals: "The son of man has authority *on earth* to forgive sins" (Mark 2:19), just as God does in heaven above. Matthew understands Mark perfectly: "they glorified God who had given such authority to *men*," including Jesus (Matt. 9:8). "Foxes have holes, and birds of the air have nests, but the son of man has no place to lay down his head" (Matt. 8:20), as the contrast with other species ought to make clear, refers to the nomadic character of human existence, which Jesus' itinerant ministry exemplifies.

The various predictions of the sufferings of the son of man would fit the category of speaking gingerly of one's own coming fate. Again, it is as if directly saying "*I am* about to go under the

---

27 Geza Vermes, *Jesus the Jew: A Historian's Reading of the Gospels* (London: Fontana/Collins, 1976), pp. 188–191.

knife" would be inviting disaster. Yes, it is superstitious, but who does not occasionally think this way?

Was "the Son of Man" used as a Messianic title in first-century Judaism? Apparently not, but *almost*. Maurice Casey[28] applied his magnifying glass on every scrap of Jewish literature that mentioned the phrase, based on Daniel chapter 7's vision of the "one like a son of man" who, fresh from his victory over an ocean full of Toho Studios *kaijus*, is enthroned at the right hand of the Ancient of Days. The one like a son of man must originally have been cloud-riding Jehovah, the white-haired ancient his Father, El Elyon. The second-century BCE Danielic author may not have known that any more than common Bible readers do today.[29] Ancient scribes *did* associate the son of man vision with the coming Messiah, but they used it as a kind of shorthand reference to that passage and the end-time victory anticipated there. But, oddly, they did not think to say the Messiah *is* the Son of Man. This applies equally to the Messianic deliverer in The Similitudes of Enoch and Fourth Ezra. This may be a case of hair-splitting, but even so, the formulaic use of the phrase seems quite closely analogous to simply using the title "Messiah." If, when you hear the one, you automatically think of the other, well, really, what is the difference?

There are, of course, several gospel sayings which speak of the Danielic Son of Man, but it is far from clear that in them Jesus is referring to himself. Obviously, in them, as in the non-Danielic uses of "son of man," he speaks of the figure in the third person, "he," not the first, "I." But if the Danielic ones have anything to do with Jesus, there is nothing to indicate it.[30] We think otherwise only because we habitually lump them in with the non-Messianic

---

[28] Maurice Casey, *Son of Man: The Interpretation and Influence of Daniel 7* (London: S.P.C.K., 1979) "The Son of Man Problem," pp. 224–240.

[29] At least Margaret Barker, *The Great Angel: A Study of Israel's Second God* (Louisville: Westminster/John Knox Press, 1992), "The Evidence of the New Testament," pp. 213–232, and Daniel Boyarin, *The Jewish Gospels: The Story of the Jewish Christ* (New York: The New Press, 2012), pp. 25–70, understand the link between pre-Deuteronomic Yahweh and Messianism. I am, however, baffled by Boyarin's dismissal of Vermes's treatment of the non-Messianic uses of "son of man."

[30] Bultmann, *Theology of the New Testament*, p. 29.

sayings: the circumlocutions and the self-justifications by appeal to the common lot of humanity. But look at them: would they read like self-references if we did not expect them to?

> Whoever in this generation of sinners and adulterers is ashamed of me and my words, of him will the Son of Man be likewise ashamed when he comes in the glory of his Father with the holy angels. (Mark 8:38)

> When the Son of Man comes, will he find any faith on earth? (Luke 18:8)

> Then they will see the Son of Man coming in clouds with great power and glory. (Mark 13:26)

> You will see the Son of Man sitting at the right hand of Power and coming with the clouds of heaven. (Mark 14:62)

> No one has ascended to heaven but he who descended from heaven, the Son of Man who is in heaven. (John 3:13)

> You will see heaven opened, and the angels of God ascending and descending upon the Son of Man. (John 2:51)

> Watch at all times, praying that you may have strength to escape all these things that will take place, and to stand before the Son of Man. (Luke 21:36)

> When the Son of Man comes in his glory, and all the angels with him, then he will sit on his glorious throne. Before him will be gathered all the nations, and he will separate them one from another as a shepherd separates the sheep from the goats, and he will place the sheep at his right hand, but the goats at the left. (Matt. 25:31–33)

My point in all this is that in all the Son of Man passages that refer to the Danielic enthronement scene, Jesus is not referring to himself, and thus, as Mark depicts him, Jesus is *not* blabbing the Messianic secret when he mentions the apocalyptic Son of Man.[31]

The Lord's Prayers

The great Christian prayer, called variously the Our Father, the Paternoster, and the Lord's Prayer, is given in two forms in Matthew and Luke. Both evangelists inherited it from the Q source. Why do they differ in the earliest manuscripts? Matthew's version is more poetic, consistently employing classic techniques of Hebrew poetry such as "synthetic parallelism," the immediate restatement of one line in paraphrased form. "The heavens declare the glory of God; the firmament showeth his handiwork" (Psalm 19:1) really mean the same thing, but the repetition provides a pleasant ringing echo. We see the same device in Matthew 6:10, "Thy kingdom come; thy will be done on earth as it is in heaven." For God's kingdom to come means that his will is finally going to be carried out among humans down here as it already is among angels up there. There is also "antithetical parallelism" where you reiterate your initial statement by offering its negative corollary: "Jehovah has sworn, and will not change his mind..." (Psalm 110:4). Likewise Matthew's Lord's Prayer has "Lead us not into temptation, but deliver us from the Evil One" (Matt. 6:13).

Luke's version (Luke 11:2–4) is shorter, lacking the parallels: just "thy kingdom come" and "lead us not into temptation." The opening address to God is short and sweet. Instead of Matthew's "Our Father who art in heaven," Luke has simply "Father." What gives? Has Matthew poetically embellished a briefer, more prosaic Q original? Or has Luke flattened out a

---

[31] Robert M. Price, "The Synoptic Apocalypse and the Son of Man" in *Journal of Higher Criticism* Vol. 15, no. 1, pp. 4–22. In view of the astonishing fact that both Josephus and Yohanon ben Zakkai nominated Vespasian as the Jewish Messiah, Joseph Atwill (*Caesar's Messiah: The Roman Conspiracy to Invent Jesus.* Flavian Signature Edition [Charleston, SC: CreateSpace, 2011]) and James S. Valliant and Warren Fahy (*Creating Christ: How Roman Emperors Invented Christianity* [Hertford, NC: Crossroad Press, 2018]) suggest that the Son of Man in Mark 13 is actually a veiled reference to Vespasian's son Titus. You do not have to buy the whole Roman origin theory to take this particular feature of it seriously.

more poetic Q original? Actually, either possibility would make sense. Luke does break up a piece of Q's poetic parallelism in Luke 12:33 (cf, Matt. 6:19–21), so it wouldn't be surprising if he did it here, too.

But the gap between the two versions actually begins to shrink as we go from the earlier to the later manuscripts. Luke's Lord's Prayer starts sounding more and more like Matthew's! If we think the process was simply one of calculated harmonization, why was it gradual, not done in one fell swoop? It looks like what happened was that, as a scribe was making a new copy of Luke, when he got to the Lord's Prayer, he went on automatic pilot, mental muscle memory, and simply wrote down the Prayer as he knew it from weekly repetition in church. The thing is: everybody liked Matthew's poetic version better, and it was standard in the liturgy. Thus Luke's text finally morphed into Matthew's with the single exception of retaining Luke's "forgive us our debts" instead of Matthew's "forgive us our trespasses."

No Gentiles Need Apply

Why did some early Jewish Christians oppose the idea of a Gentile Mission? Why withhold the message of salvation? That seems pretty hard-hearted, mean-spirited, right? Let 'em all go to hell (maybe in a hand basket, maybe not)! But no. You see, though admittedly there were Jews understandably bitter at the treatment they had long received at Gentile hands and relished the thought of their oppressors writhing in hell, officially Judaism did not blame Gentiles for not being Jews. Jews considered Gentiles righteous if they kept the modest collection of basic Noahic laws stipulated for all mankind in Genesis 9. If they were not Jews, they were not obliged to keep the Jewish Torah. Granted, Jews figured the odds of their pagan neighbors actually being righteous were not good because of their degraded polytheism, but it was possible. Furthermore, Isaiah 2:1–4 and Micah 4:1–2 had predicted that one day, when God vindicated his people, the Gentiles would say, "What do you know? Looks like those Jews were right all along! To hell with Mithras! Let's sign up for Jewish catechism class!"

(Many Gentiles already felt that way and began attending synagogue.)

It is likely the moss-back Jerusalem elders in Acts chapter 10, who were affronted at Peter preaching to the Roman Cornelius and his household, believed that God would redeem the Gentiles in his own sweet time, as Isaiah and Micah had said.[32] In the same way, Presbyterians were contentiously divided over whether to join in the great world-wide Protestant Missionary crusade of the nineteenth century. If the Almighty needed the help of mere mortals to get the job done, he would ask for it. Nothing Western missionaries could do would affect God's primordial allotment of the elect and the reprobate.

But often our theologies, and the policies they dictate, turn out not to match reality. (Ask the dejected Millerites and the insecticide-gargling snake-handlers.) And when reality intervenes, we have to make mid-course corrections. Even so, Gentile "God-fearers," already flirting with Judaism, began showing up for Christian baptism: "Ready or not, here I come!"

I mentioned the story of Peter opening up the mission to Gentiles in Acts 10–11. It is presented as a significant departure from then-traditional practice. What authorization did Peter claim for his shocking actions? There were two. First we read that Peter dreamed that God lowered a huge canvas sheet before him, containing all manner of animals, kosher and non-kosher. The heavenly voice told him, "Go ahead, Peter! Kill and eat!" What? Even the pigs and lobsters? No way, *Lord*![33] But God replied, "Who do you think de*creed* those kosher laws? Do you think you're holier than *me*?"

Second, downstairs, servants of Cornelius (whose friends no doubt called him "Corny") are at the door asking for him. Peter goes with them, greets the Gentiles, and starts preaching. He doesn't get far when the Holy Spirit, apparently a bit impatient (as most of us probably are during sermons), engulfs the group,

---

[32] Joachim Jeremias, *Jesus' Promise to the Nations*. Trans. S.H. Hooke. Franz Delitzsch Lectures for 1953. Studies in Biblical Theology No. 24 (London: SCM Press, 1967).

[33] I love the irony! "Why do you call me Lord and do not do what I say?"

causing them to burst into glossolalic ecstasy, just like on the Day of Pentecost! It was like the time some guy sharing a train compartment with evangelist Charles Spurgeon asked him if he believed in infant baptism, and Spurgeon replied, "*Believe* in it? Why, man, I haven't *seen* it!"

But apparently the Holy Spirit's say-so was not good enough for *some* people. So there arose various attempts to anchor the Gentile Mission back during the ministry of Jesus. Mark 7:24–30 has Jesus vacationing in the old Philistine territory of Tyre and Sidon, but, despite the sunglasses and false nose, he is quickly recognized by an intrusive fan, a woman who begs him to exorcize her demoniac daughter (resembling, I suspect, a young Linda Blair). Jesus, irritated, tells her to beat it; only fellow Jews are entitled to his healing power. If he were to grant her request he would be taking the kids' birthday cake and feeding it to the dogs. Ouch! It looks to me like this is a Socratic pose, raising the bar to see just how serious she is. And she is. Quick-witted, she counters: "True, true, but do not the kids slip cake crumbs to the pets under the table?" This is what Jesus must have been hoping for. "*Touché!* Just for that, lady, you have got your healing." When mom gets home, what do you know? Little Regan is fine!

Matthew 8:5–13 and the parallel in Luke 7:1–7 feature a similar sequence, only this time Jesus is home in Capernaum when a Roman centurion (in Matthew) or the centurion's representatives (Luke)[34] come to call. The officer has a slave at home who is like a son to him, and is in a bad way. Would Jesus consider curing him? Just as the Sanhedrinists decline to enter Pilate's palace so to preserve ritual purity, the centurion prevents Jesus from visiting his home lest he become similarly defiled. Jesus confesses himself amazed at this goy's faith! It will win him a place at the soon-coming Marriage Supper of the Lamb. And certain Jews will find themselves conspicuously absent from the occasion. Bultmann

---

[34] It looks to me like Luke has let his planned Cornelius story in Acts 10 rub off on his version of the centurion's servant. In both, unlike Matthew, Luke has a friendly Roman centurion send his subordinates to seek the help of the Jewish holy man. Is this another contradiction? Of course it is, though who cares but neurotic inerrantists?

theorized that these are two variants of a single original story.[35] Well, they're not anymore, so who cares? But both are attempts to retroactively recruit Jesus as an endorser of the Gentile Mission. Note that in both cases, Jesus heals/saves a *Gentile child* at a *distance*. The sick person represents Gentiles of *the next generation* and *at a physical remove* from Jesus/from Palestine. They stand for Gentiles in the future who, in Greece, Rome, or Asia Minor, will embrace the gospel message. Both stories even include overt Gentile Mission sloganeering: "Truly, I say to you, not even in Israel have I found such faith. I tell you, many will come from east and west and sit at table with Abraham, Isaac, and Jacob in the kingdom of heaven" (Matt. 8:10–11; cf, Luke 7:9, "I tell you, not even in Israel have I found such faith.").

Matthew 15:24–27's version of the Mark 7 story of the Syro-Phoenician woman is especially revealing: "He answered, 'I was sent only to the lost sheep of the house of Israel. But she came and knelt before him, saying, 'Lord, help me.' And he answered, 'It is not fair to take the children's bread and throw it to the dogs.' She said, 'Yes, Lord, yet even the dogs eat the crumbs that fall from their masters' table.'" You see? Jesus first spouts the slogan of the "Israel Only" faction, only to have the Gentile woman refute him, i.e. his policy also quoted in Matthew 10:5: just Jews. Some manuscripts have Jesus say, "Let the children be fed," while others have added the word "first," implying that some scribe has altered the original "Israel Only" factional slogan in favor of his own, pro-Gentile Mission position: "the gospel… is the power of God for salvation to every one who has faith, to the Jew *first* and also to the Greek" (Rom. 1:16).

Now to turn to the much-discussed passage Matthew 10:5–6. It stands in tension with, no, in contradiction to, the Great Commission that concludes the Gospel of Matthew:

Go therefore and make disciples of all nations, baptizing them in the name of the Father and of the Son and of the Holy Spirit, teaching them to observe all that I have commanded you; and lo, I am with you always, to the close of the age."

---

[35] Bultmann, *History of the Synoptic Tradition*, p. 38.

Compare this with the Not-So-Great Commission:

> These twelve Jesus sent out, charging them, "Go nowhere among the Gentiles, and enter no town of the Samaritans, but go rather to the lost sheep of the house of Israel....When they persecute you in one town, flee to the next; for truly, I say to you, you will not have gone through all the towns of Israel, before the Son of man comes. (Matt. 10:5–6, 23)

Albert Schweitzer did not yet see what the form critics would soon be pointing out, that the individual units of gospel tradition were artificially placed in the sequence in which we now read them.[36] Schweitzer assumed that Matthew was pretty much an accurate account of events as they had occurred. Accordingly, he supposed that Jesus sent the disciples out to herald the near-immediate coming of Doomsday, and told them to make it snappy, since it would not be possible to cover even the sum of the villages of Israel before the axe fell. The Great Tribulation should erupt; Jesus himself should be transfigured, like Enoch, into the superhuman Son of Man. Imagine his surprise when the twelve returned to a world (and a Jesus) unchanged! Back to the drawing board to draft a new plan of salvation: his atoning crucifixion.

This is strikingly ingenious but now easy to recognize as erroneous. There never was a moment when Jesus expected the mission of the twelve to coincide with the end of the world and was disappointed that the whole thing fizzled. Rather, we can see that the chapter 10 commission is exactly parallel to the chapter 28 commission. Both specify the intended mission field. Both envision the mission lasting until the end of the age. They are competing mission charges, one from the Israel Only faction, the other from the Gentile Mission faction. No one thought the Matthew 10 version was intended as temporary, to be superseded by the Matthew 28 version. The presence of both in the same gospel merely attests the composite, compromise character of the

---

[36] Karl Ludwig Schmidt, *The Place of the Gospels in the General History of Literature*. Trans. Byron R. McCane (Columbia: University of South Carolina, 2002).

Gospel of Matthew, written for and by the pluralistic congregation at Antioch.[37] Like the church at Rome as we observe it in the Epistle to the Romans; it mediates between Jewish and Gentile factions, granting ground to each in hopes of co-existence. Sometimes the best option is to juxtapose rival positions, respected but not reconciled.

Itinerant Inventory

Something most of us seldom notice (because who cares?) is the difference between the items permitted the itinerants as they trod the dusty roads preaching and prophesying in the name of Jesus. The sets of instructions embedded in all three Synoptic gospels (two in Luke!) were originally formulated to govern the conduct of early Christian missioners, not for the personal disciples of Jesus. Indeed we should consider the missions on which Jesus is said to have sent them mere retrojections of the ministries of post-Jesus charismatics [38](as in 3 John and Matthew 25:31–8). In any case, the lists differ.

Mark 6:7–11 allows a walking stick, a pair of sandals, and a single cloak, but no bread, no pouch, and no money, no GPS unit. Matthew 10:9–10 subtracts even the sandals and walking stick but allows a single tunic and mentions no cloaks. Does this mean Matthew thought Mark was not being strict enough? Luke 9:1–3 omits any mention of footwear but bans walking sticks, pouches, food, and money. Luke has a thing about walking sticks, too. Again, only one tunic is allowed. Luke 10:4 has "no purse, no bag, no sandals" (cf, Luke 22:35) but mentions nothing else, plus or minus. All the lists presuppose that the itinerants can expect largesse from those to whom they preach, obviously those who do not slam the door in their faces. In short, the sheep, not the goats, can be relied on to supply their needs. The basic asceticism of the

---

[37] Again, see my article "Antioch's Aftershocks."

[38] Gerd Theissen, "The Wandering Radicals: Light Shed by the Sociology of Literature on the Early Transmission of Jesus Sayings." In Theissen, *Social Reality and the Early Christians: Theology, Ethics, and the New Testament.* Trans. Margaret Kohl (Minneapolis: Fortress Press, 1992), pp. 33–59.

regimen facilitates travelling light as well necessitating faith in God's providence. Their accoutrement is quite similar to the dress and equipment of their competitors, the Cynic itinerants with whom they were often and easily confused, and this may be why certain items have been forbidden, to distinguish the Christian vagabonds from their look-alike rivals who sported a uniform of cloak, pouch, and staff. [39]

But the differences are so picky, we might guess that the evangelists did not bother keeping the details straight. We see this especially with Luke. His first list applies, as far as the narrative is concerned, to the twelve as they canvass Palestine, while the second list pertains to the (certainly imaginary) mission of the seventy, an intra-diegetic precedent for the Gentile Mission (seventy missioners for the traditional seventy nations). Why would the instructions for the twelve and those for the seventy differ? The second seems like a hasty summary of the first. This implies that the ministry of the itinerants is well in the past. This is made explicit in Luke 22:35–36. The lists, along with the Mission Charge passages in which they appear, survived in the tradition because Christian itinerants were guided by them (and also no doubt liked to point to them to brag to their hosts that they were following the strict regimen of Jesus and thus deserved generous support). But this is over by the time the gospels were written, and the material has become merely ostensible hagiographic data about the Blessed Apostles.

Persecution Sooner or Later?

In John 16:1–2 John makes his Jesus character predict a time of persecution of Christians. For them it lies in the future. But wait a minute! Did not chapter 9, verse 22, of the same gospel say that such persecution had already begun in Jesus' time? In both passages, the persecution is specified as excommunication from the synagogue (at least for starters). This is a pretty blatant contradiction all right. But it is easy to account for, and the

---

[39] F. Gerald Downing, *Cynics and Christian Origins* (Edinburgh: T&T Clark, 1992), p. 32.

explanation shows that it is not a question of someone's stupid goof.

We have seen that in the Gospel of John history is at the service of theology. Here is another instance of it. The anachronisms of John result from the narrative strategy of having "Jesus" predict the conditions of the evangelist's own day (and that of his intended readers) *and* imposing those later conditions on the characters in the narrative, Jesus' contemporaries: what would Jesus have done? Another example is what Jesus says in his Last Supper discourse about his future replacement by the Paraclete:

> I have yet many things to say to you, but you cannot bear them now. When the Spirit of truth comes, he will guide you into all the truth; for he will not speak on his own authority, but whatever he hears he will speak, and he will declare to you the things that are to come. He will glorify me, for he will take what is mine and declare it to you. All that the Father has is mine; therefore I said that he will take what is mine and declare it to you. (John 16:12–15)

This is presented as another prediction of something that had not yet occurred but that should be expected. And yet it could not be clearer that it has already happened: this is why the Jesus in the Gospel of John sounds so different in every way from the Jesus of the Synoptics. John is filled with mystical and Christological discourse conspicuously absent from Matthew, Mark, and Luke. The fourth evangelist knows full well that his Jesus is not teaching the same stuff as the other Jesus books, and in chapter 16 John explains why, at least to anyone who has ears to hear. And such readers will have no difficulty with this "contradiction."

5

Miracles

Did Jesus *Do* Miracles?

The question here is not whether a/the historical Jesus actually performed miracles, but only what to make of the fact that some gospel material seems to deny that he did, while other gospel texts depict numerous wonders. There is no need to review or to enumerate the marvels ascribed to Jesus. We need only consider a single astonishing text, Mark 8:11–12.

> The Pharisees came and began to argue with him, seeking from him a sign from heaven, to test him. And he sighed deeply in his spirit, and said, "Why does this generation seek a sign? Truly, I say to you, no sign shall be given to this generation."

Oh what Olympic gymnastics we see conservative exegetes executing when they find themselves cornered by this frightening passage! "It *cannot* mean what it obviously means! Er, I mean...." Uh, maybe Jesus just meant that, though he did in fact constantly perform miracles, he refused to perform one on demand. In the film *The Last Temptation of Christ*, Pontius Pilate asks the captive Jesus to perform one of his rumored miracles (usurping Herod Antipas' lines from Luke 23:8), and Jesus answers that he is not some trained circus animal. The point is that Jesus performs miracles in response to faith, not to skepticism. A good point, as Luke also notes in 16:31: "If they do not hear Moses and the prophets, neither will they be convinced if someone should rise from the dead."

But this does not resolve our dilemma. Jesus' answer to his critics in Mark is not that he refuses to do a miracle *for them*, on *this particular occasion*. Rather, *this generation* will see no miracles from him. The intended point would seem exactly parallel to that of 1 Corinthians 1:22–24.

> For Jews demand signs and Greeks seek wisdom, but we preach Christ crucified, a stumbling block to Jews and folly to Gentiles, but to those who are called, both Jews and Greeks, Christ the power of God and the wisdom of God.

These Jews who want to settle theological claims by means of attesting miracles would include Mark's skeptical Pharisees. And, like Mark's Jesus, 1 Corinthians 1's Paul regrets that he must disappoint such demands. Unless you can come up with something better, I have to say that both passages deny that Jesus performed miracles. Had Paul known of any miracles done by Jesus, would he not have produced them? He never mentions any, after all. And even if he knew of some wonders wrought by Jesus but refused to acknowledge them, why? Would that mean he found fault with Jesus' policy?

It is clear that subsequent Christians who believed Jesus *had* done miracles had a serious problem with the implications of the Markan original. Let us see how they embellished it in order to remove its theological sting.

> An evil and adulterous generation seeks for a sign, but no sign shall be given to it *except the sign of Jonah.* (Matt.16:4)

> When the crowds were increasing, he began to say, "This generation is an evil generation; it seeks a sign, but no sign shall be given to it *except the sign of Jonah. For as Jonah became a sign to the men of Nineveh, so will the Son of man be to this generation."* (Luke 11:30)

> Then some of the scribes and Pharisees said to him, "Teacher, we wish to see a sign from you." But he answered them, "An evil and adulterous generation seeks for a sign; but no sign shall be given to it *except the sign of the prophet Jonah. For as Jonah was three days and three nights in the belly of the whale, so will the Son of man be three days and three nights in the*

heart of the earth. The men of Nineveh will arise at the judgment with this generation and condemn it; for they repented at the preaching of Jonah, and behold, something greater than Jonah is here." (Matt. 12:38–41)

It is easy to count the tree rings. Matthew 16:4 adds "but the sign of Jonah," whatever he thought that meant—if anything. It is like his "correction" of Mark's Jordan baptism story. John the Baptist expresses the unease felt by Matthew himself at the prospect of Jesus undergoing a baptism of repentance. Should not *Jesus* be baptizing *John*? But Jesus "explains" that "It behooves us to fulfill all righteousness." All that seems to mean is, "Do not worry; this is not what it *looks* like!" In the same way, "the sign of Jonah" is no more than a negation of Jesus' refusal ever to perform miracles.

But others were not satisfied with that. An answer is not an answer if you cannot understand it. So Luke 11:30 helps a little: Jonah *was* a sign in his day. Something he was or did is reflected or repeated by Jesus centuries later. Jonah was the "type;" Jesus was the antitype. But in what way? Just that both were preaching repentance and judgment to their contemporaries? Would that be considered a "sign"? Would you not expect something a bit more spectacular? The evangelist Matthew, like Mithras, took the bull by the horns: he zeroed in on Jonah's one famous feat: surviving getting swallowed by Leviathan. Why not make that a foreshadowing of Jesus being "swallowed" by the grave and emerging alive? Fair enough; one only wonders why it took so long for someone to think of it! But that only holds for the first "sign of Jonah" version, not for Mark's original.

Yes, Mark 8:11–12 does rule out any gospel miracles. But then what about all those healings, exorcisms, etc.? How do we account for them? Faith created them, not the faith exercised by those Jesus heals ("Your faith has made you well."), but the faith of early Christians who magnified their Savior by dreaming up super feats to glorify him. The same thing happened with the Prophet Muhammad, who had to meet the challenge of skeptics, not with miracles, but with excuses (Koran 13:27: "Those who disbelieve say, 'If only a portent were sent down upon him from his Lord' Lo, Allah sendeth whom he will astray, and guideth unto himself all who turn unto him"). Nonetheless, many miracles were later ascribed to him. Similarly, seventeenth-century Messiah Sabbatai Sevi was the hero of many miracle stories spread by popular imagination despite the early caution of his forerunner, Nathan of Gaza, who informed Israel that they would have to believe without the evidence of miracles.[1]

Double the Demoniacs!

Mark 5:1–20 presents us with perhaps the most exciting adventure of Jesus as a mythic hero (based on two episodes from Homer's *Odyssey*, Circe's transformation of Odysseus' soldiers into squealing pigs, and Odysseus' encounter with the fearsome Cyclops Polyphemus).[2] The story is well known: Jesus and his men enter the Gentile district of the Ten Cities (Decapolis) on the opposite side of the Lake of Galilee, where they are at once accosted by a naked, towering hulk covered in bruises and festering cuts, broken manacles trailing along behind him. He is possessed by thousands ("legions") of demons, apparently the ghosts of those interred in the abandoned cemetery where he dwells. He needs no introduction to Jesus, whom he, or rather his besetting devils, already knows on sight. He is in a panic, surmising that Jesus, God's wretched do-gooder, has come at an hour the demons expected not and is there to confine them in the Great Abyss, right next to the Titans and the fifty-headed Giants. No fair! And presumably they are correct! Jesus has come to put an end to their mischief. But the Son of God is open to negotiation. He grants their proposal, transferring them from the man, collapsing now like a popped balloon, and into a herd of pigs grazing on a nearby hillside. The unfortunate shoats go wild at the invasion of spirits even more unclean than they and plunge, lemming-like, into the lake! As the reader is apparently supposed

---

[1] Gershom Scholem, *Sabbatai Sevi the Mystical Messiah*. Trans. R.J. Zwi Werblowsky. (Princeton: Princeton University Press, 1973), p. 211: "I was told that Israel ought to believe [in the messiah] without any sign or miracle."

[2] Dennis R. MacDonald. *The Homeric Epics and the Gospel of Mark* (New Haven: Yale University Press, 2000),"Speluncular Savages," pp. 63–76.

to know, the half-mythological Sea (the Old Testament Yamm) is what H.P. Lovecraft called "the ante-chamber of Hell." So the Lethal Legion has outsmarted themselves! Little did they realize their bargaining would win them only a thrill-ride into the very Abyss they hoped to avoid!

After a quick trip to the Gerasene Men's Shop to get the ex-demoniac a new suit, he is ready, he thinks, to greet the local populace who have come to investigate the ruckus, which could be heard all the way back to town. But when they recognize him, albeit shaven, clean and pressed, the villagers are more frightened than ever! And not of *him*, but of Jesus! Anybody who could take on the neighborhood demoniac and beat him may pose an even greater danger! Seeing that he is still *persona non grata*, the former Frankenstein pleads with Jesus to let him aboard as the disciples begin climbing into the boat. It is not safe for him in Gerasa! But he now finds demon-relief has come at a price: he has missionary work to do! Jesus sends him among the very people who fear him, to attest the grace of God toward him. Remember, the Decapolitans are Gentile pagans (raising *pigs*, after all) and could use some Jehovah witnessing.

Sometimes we read that the episode seems to imply that the Messianic secret does not apply outside Jewish territory, since, among fellow Jews, Jesus attempts to prevent his patients from publicizing his cures. Why not here? I think a better explanation of this apparent contradiction is that Jesus tells the ex-Legionnaire to tell people what "the Lord, i.e. Jehovah," has done for him (Mark 5:19), but *instead* the fellow credits the miracle to *Jesus* himself (Mark 5:20). So much for the secret![3]

Luke's version (Luke 8:26–39) is basically the same as the Markan original, though it is noteworthy that Luke eliminates any ambiguity as to whom Jesus told the man to credit his good fortune: Luke says he is to "declare how much *God* has done for

---

[3] I find it just hilarious that Evangelical apologists insist that the gospels must be accurate because the apostles would have functioned like Snopes fact-checkers ferreting out fake "Jesus" sayings/stories and censoring them—when the gospels tell us that when Jesus himself attempted to prevent (true!) stories of himself from spreading *he could not do it!*

him." Not Jesus. But he disobeys. I think Luke correctly understood Mark's version and wanted to make sure we did, too.

John's gospel notoriously lacks any and all exorcisms except the big one: his imminent casting out the Archon of this World, Satan (John 12:31). So there is no Gerasene demoniac in John. But that is okay, since Matthew has *two* of them! The story runs the same, as in both other Synoptics, except, where Mark and Luke depict a single possessed man, Matthew has *two* of them, and to no apparent purpose. The second one is as absolutely colorless, just as much an empty shadow, as John son of Zebedee in Acts chapter 8. What is he doing there? Nothing much. For all the vexation he causes for inerrancy harmonists, it might as well be worth it. But it is not. Popular fundamentalism seems (guiltily) satisfied with saying that, while there were actually two of these monsters, Mark and Luke each put the spotlight on his favorite! Let me guess: Mark had a special affinity for Gog, Luke for Magog. Strauss ridicules such shenanigans:

> It is astonishing how long harmonists have resorted to miserable expedients, such as that Mark and Luke mention only one because he was particularly distinguished by wildness, or Matthew [mentions] two, because he included the attendant who guarded the maniac, rather than admit an essential difference between the two narratives.[4]

Strauss wrote in 1835, but such tortured gimmicks were still alive and well in 1927. "Matthew says there were two demoniacs. Mark and Luke mention only one probably because he was the more violent of the two, and [their] spokesman."[5]

Strauss had a bit more patience with another proposed solution: "the addition of a second demoniac by Matthew has been explained by supposing the plurality of the demons spoken of in the narratives became in his apprehension a plurality of

---

[4] Strauss, *Life of Jesus,* p. 425.

[5] Henry H. Halley, *Halley's Bible Handbook: An Abbreviated Bible Commentary* (Grand Rapids: Zondervan Publishing House, 24th ed., 1965), p. 467.

demoniacs."[6] In fact, something of the kind appears to have happened in the case of another exorcism tale, that of the Ephesian Wild Man (which I think was a retelling of this one). Acts 19:14 tells us that a squad of Ghostbusters tried to cast out a particularly pugnacious demon who was, however, not impressed with their efforts. The demoniac administered a whuppin', ripping their clothes off and bruising *both* of them good! "Both" of them, you say? Were there not *seven*? No; as Hugh J. Schonfeld[7] pointed out, these guys were known as "the Sons of Sceva," this last being the same as the Greek number seven. Some scribe, nodding at his scriptorium, garbled an original reading, "the Sons of Sceva" into "the seven sons."

This is but one instance of Matthew doubling things, e.g., he clones Mark's Bartimaeus character (Mark 10:46–52; Matt. 20:29–34), again, to no apparent purpose. Is it possible that Matthew somehow misunderstood Mark 10:46's "Bartimaeus, son of Timaeus" as the names of two different men, Bartimaeus and his dad, plain old Timaeus? I doubt it, but I do not have anything that sounds better. And it gets even weirder! Matthew 9:27–31 is the *exact same* story, again with *another* two blind men, only this time neither is given a name.

By the way, the Bartimaeus anecdote affords another headache for inerrantists. Matthew 20:29 has Jesus healing the blind beggar on his way *out of* the city of Jericho, while Luke 18:35–43 has it happen on the way *in*! Uh-oh! Give me another handful of Excedrin! But actually, the solution is pretty simple: both Matthew and Luke are dependent on the earlier Gospel of Mark which says Jesus entered Jericho but then left it, along the way restoring the blind man's sight. Both subsequent evangelists decided to trim Mark's text of incidentals. Luke chopped the mention of Jesus leaving the city, giving the impression that Jesus performed the healing as he was heading into the town. Matthew did the opposite. No big deal!

----

[6] Strauss, *Life of Jesus*, p. 425.

[7] Hugh J. Schonfield, *The Authentic New Testament* (New American Library/A Mentor Book, 1958), p. 228, n. 142.

One more case of Matthean doubling: did Jesus ride *one* or *two* donkeys into Jerusalem? Mark, Luke, and John have, of course, Jesus riding on a donkey into Jerusalem. It is a pure-bred donkey, not some crummy hybrid mule. That is what Zechariah meant by "a donkey, even the foal of a donkey." But Matthew balances his Jesus on the backs of two donkeys, one smaller than the other. Never mind how Jesus managed to do this; how did the *evangelist* come to do this? Strange as the result seems, the anomaly is easy to explain. It reflects a major development in Jewish hermeneutics. The rabbis fully understood the nature and use of poetic parallelism and continued to employ the technique in their own poetic and liturgical compositions. But they came to the point of thinking such language unbecoming and incompatible with the Bible as a product of divine inspiration.

> The rabbinic exegete… is "blind" to parallelism by conviction and temperament. The text's holiness both allows and requires him to search out the highest possible meaning of a verse. Repetition, rhetoric, emphasis—these are traits best not attributed to the word of God, all the more so because "searching" a verse through its canonized surroundings will yield so much richer a meaning.[8]

This means that Matthew, a Jewish-Christian scribe (Matt. 13:52), did not feel at liberty to treat Zechariah 9:9 ("Behold, your king is coming to you. He is just and endowed with salvation, Humble, and mounted on a donkey, even on a colt, the foal of a donkey") as the poetry it obviously is. Like his scribal colleagues, he felt obliged to treat the text as prose, in order to squeeze more "information" out of it. The result is grotesque, comical, but not according to these ancient standards. (But I doubt Everett F. Harrison had anything like this in mind!)

I cannot resist pointing something out here: there is a surprising analogy between what Matthew has done with Zechariah 9:9 and what fundamentalist harmonists do with

---

[8] James L. Kugel, *The Idea of Biblical Poetry: Parallelism and Its History* (Baltimore: Johns Hopkins Press, 1992), p. 139.

contradictory passages. In their different ways, both are allowing their *a priori* beliefs about what is or is not fitting for inspired scripture to limit and control their reading of the text, often in drastically implausible, even ridiculous, ways. Is there not something wrong here?

Mister Beal Meets His Match[9]

Did Jesus cast out demons by invoking Beelzebul, as his critics charged? Mark, Luke, and Matthew call it slander, so where is the contradiction? This time the conflict is between the extant texts and the Q source underlying Matthew and Luke. Compare the canonical versions of the three Synoptics. Mark 3:22–30 has:

> And the scribes who came down from Jerusalem said, "He is possessed by Beelzebul, and by the prince of demons he casts out the demons." And he called them to him, and said to them in parables, *"How can Satan cast out Satan?* If a kingdom is divided against itself, that kingdom cannot stand. And if a house is divided against itself, that house will not be able to stand. And if Satan has risen up against himself and is divided, he cannot stand, but is coming to an end. But no one can enter a strong man's house and plunder his goods, unless he first binds the strong man; then indeed he may plunder his house."

Matthew 12:22–32 reads:

> Then a blind and dumb demoniac was brought to him, and he healed him, so that the dumb man spoke and saw. And all the people were amazed, and said, "Can this be the Son of David?" But when the Pharisees heard it they said, "It is only by Beelzebul, the prince of demons, that this man casts out demons." Knowing their thoughts, he said to them, "Every kingdom divided against itself is laid waste, and no city or

---

[9] That is the title of episode 111 of *Father Knows Best* (December 11, 1957) in which Margaret wards off the Devil who is trying to take Dad's soul. It scared the hell out of me as a little kid! Written by Ed James and Roswell Rogers.

house divided against itself will stand; and if Satan casts out Satan, he is divided against himself; how then will his kingdom stand? *And if I cast out demons by Beelzebul, by whom do your sons cast them out? Therefore they shall be your judges. But if it is by the Spirit of God that I cast out demons, then the kingdom of God has come upon you.* Or how can one enter a strong man's house and plunder his goods, unless he first binds the strong man? Then indeed he may plunder his house."

Luke 11:14–22 is similar:

Now he was casting out a demon that was dumb; when the demon had gone out, the dumb man spoke, and the people marveled. But some of them said, "He casts out demons by Beelzebul, the prince of demons;" while others, to test him, sought from him a sign from heaven. But he, knowing their thoughts, said to them, "Every kingdom divided against itself is laid waste, and a divided household falls. *And if Satan also is divided against himself, how will his kingdom stand? For you say that I cast out demons by Beelzebul. And if I cast out demons by Beelzebul, by whom do your sons cast them out? Therefore they shall be your judges. But if it is by the finger of God that I cast out demons, then the kingdom of God has come upon you.* When a strong man, fully armed, guards his own palace, his goods are in peace; but when one stronger than he assails him and overcomes him, he takes away his armor in which he trusted, and divides his spoil."

Try bracketing the italicized text in each version. Mark lacks the business about Jesus being no worse than "your boys" and the counter that his exorcisms presage the dawn of the kingdom of God. The Q material shared by Matthew and Luke has these items but lacks Mark's rhetorical question, "Can Satan cast out Satan?" It looks to me as if both the Q compiler and the evangelist Mark felt the need to modify the basic anecdote that found its way into both Mark and Q. And if you omit both of these modifications, what have you got left? I would say it reads like a *defense* of casting out demons by invoking Beelzebub! What else do you think the "binding of the strong man" refers to? Exorcists bound Beelzebul in order to force him to give up his "possessions." i.e. the possessed! Beelzebul naturally does not wish to see his kingdom fall, but he can do nothing to stop it, since the exorcist, in this case Jesus, has managed to bind him to his service, like Abraham defeating the kings of the cities of the plains to free his nephew Lot, who was being held hostage (Gen. 14:11–16).

Thus for Jesus to "cast out demons by Beelzebul" does not mean he is a diabolist or a confederate of the devil. It means he has *overpowered* him. Now Beelzebul must obey Jesus. Why was this suppressed in the gospel tradition? For the same reason that Matthew and Luke snipped out the Markan Jesus' Aramaic conjurations *Ephphatha* (Mark 7:34) and *Talitha Cumi* (Mark 5:41) and his magical healing gestures like spitting on the tied-up tongue and using his index fingers to unplug the ears of the deaf (Mark 7:33).[10] Jesus does not require techniques or tonics; he does what he does because he is the incarnate Word of God. "He saith unto a thing, 'Be!' and it is!"

I Don't Give a Fig

I have already mentioned Mark's practice of "sandwiching" (or intercalation, or imbrication), whereby he made two stories comment on one another by inserting one in the middle of the other or splitting each one and arranging them in an A,B,A,B pattern. Mark 11:11–21 is an instance of the latter:

And he entered Jerusalem, and went into the temple; and when he had looked round at everything, as it was already late, he went out to Bethany with the twelve. *On the following day, when they came from Bethany, he was hungry. And seeing in the distance a fig tree in leaf, he went to see if he could find*

---

[10] John 9:6–7 shows Jesus using these gimmicks to heal a blind man, which may appear incongruous for this most sophisticated gospel, but it seems the writer was willing to retain it since he could get a little mileage out of Jesus *sending* him to wash off in the Pool of Siloam, which means "sent," reminiscent both of Jesus *sending* him there to complete the process and of Jesus himself as the beloved Son whom God *sent* into the world.

anything on it. When he came to it, he found nothing but leaves, for it was not the season for figs. And he said to it, "May no one ever eat fruit from you again." And his disciples heard it. And they came to Jerusalem. And he entered the temple and began to drive out those who sold and those who bought in the temple, and he overturned the tables of the money-changers and the seats of those who sold pigeons; and he would not allow anyone to carry anything through the temple. And he taught, and said to them, "Is it not written, 'My house shall be called a house of prayer for all the nations'? But you have made it 'a den of robbers.'" And the chief priests and the scribes heard it and sought a way to destroy him; for they feared him, because all the multitude was astonished at his teaching. And when evening came they went out of the city. *As they passed by in the morning, they saw the fig tree withered away to its roots. And Peter remembered and said to him, "Master, look! The fig tree which you cursed has withered!"*

By itself, the fig tree story looks like another refugee from the apocryphal infancy/childhood gospel tradition. Young Jesus is hungry and expects a fig tree to help him out, but no such luck; it happens to be the off-season for figs, which the tree cannot help. So, in a fit of pique, the impetuous Savior zaps the poor thing. It's like when we fall victim to a door slamming shut on us and we retaliate by kicking it! It is kind of embarrassing, so someone has tried to redeem the silly tale by tacking on an utterly ill-fitting platitude about the miracle-working power of faith (Mark 11:22–26). A much better attempt to dignify the fig tree folktale is the Markan sandwich, which makes the withering of the tree a symbol of the fruitless bankruptcy of formal temple worship and commercialism—and resulting destruction to come!

Matthew undoes Mark's sandwich, as when we pry off the lid of an Oreo cookie so we can lick the filling first. Or maybe he had independent access to the original and decided he liked the intact version better. Either way, we cannot have both Matthew's and Mark's versions be literally factual, even if we are willing to countenance the miraculous. I am unaware of any apologist contending that Jesus really killed *two* fig trees that day, one shriveling on the spot, the other taking longer, to be seen the next day, but I would not be too surprised if I did. I do not mean to ridicule someone for something they are not doing. That is not my point. But would this not be your alternative if you were affronted by the notion of one gospel writer tinkering with the work of another one? Which do you think is better? A way of interpreting the text that provides a reasonable solution to a puzzling problem? Or one that actually *creates* problems (e.g. cringe-inducing, far-fetched harmonizations)? And if you have to "rescue" the Bible's "authority" by constantly patching it up, I suggest it is time to go back to the drawing board. Believe me, I have been there.

Cartoon Physics in Action!

Let us assume Jesus really did walk on water (though those stories of the Buddha and Pythagoras doing the same thing are legendary bunk, of course!). After all, we would not want to be guilty of harboring "naturalistic presuppositions," now would we? The question before us is whether Peter, too, defied gravity.

Mark and John both tell the story of Jesus walking on the sea, which some think was originally a resurrection appearance story in which, just as in the Johannine Appendix (John 21), the disciples recognize Jesus at a distance on the shore of the Sea of Galilee/Lake of Tiberius. They are astonished because, the last they knew, he was dead! Mark's walking on water story could legitimately be read as saying they saw Jesus walking on top of the water *or* on the beach *by* the water, since the pronoun *epi* can mean either one. Again, if the latter meaning were intended, the amazement of the disciples in the boat would be due to seeing the recently crucified Jesus alive again. That is why they first think/fear that what they are seeing is a ghost—the ghost of the dead Jesus.

But Matthew is reading it with the first possibility in mind, so, for Matthew, Jesus is not defying the *grave* but defying *gravity*. In this case, they imagine Jesus to be a ghost drifting above the waves because, if a living man, he must sink. Matthew's sequel presupposes this latter understanding, which is why (only) in Matthew Peter asks Jesus to prove his identity as the living Jesus by causing Peter to join him on the lake's surface: Peter knows *he* is no ectoplasmic phantom, so if Jesus can make *him* walk on the water, too, that will show that Jesus need not be a spook either.

And Jesus obliges him. This must have been the extent of the first redactor's expansion of Mark. As we have seen, he held Peter and the twelve in higher regard than Mark did, who repeatedly depicted the disciples as uncomprehending buffoons (because he belonged to a faction, probably Paulinist, which repudiated the figureheads of a rival sect). But a subsequent Matthean redactor who wanted to take Peter back down a peg, added a new continuation.[11] Matthew 14:29 had capped off the incident with Peter successfully walking on the sea all the way to Jesus (something cleverly disguised by the "translators" of the evangelical-leaning New International Version's "came toward Jesus" in order to harmonize it with what immediately follows). But now it starts up again: Peter, midway to his goal, like Wile E. Coyote in a Roadrunner cartoon, suddenly realizes nothing is holding him up! High School Physics kicks in, and he begins to sink like the stone he is named for! Formerly Peter was pictured as a second Jesus, beside him atop the waves, like Stalin standing next to Lenin in a Soviet propaganda poster. Or like Supergirl posing beside her cousin Superman. But now Pete is back to being the oft-rescued Jimmy Olsen. Not a good look for the Prince of Apostles!

But it is not *only* mud-slinging. The adjunct to the story is a brilliant piece of homiletics. I would bet my life (or, come to think of it, maybe just yours) that every single sermon ever preached on this text used it to symbolize the Christian experience: you may be wavering, in danger of sinking into life's tossing sea of troubles. As long as you keep focused on Jesus you will make it through just fine. But perhaps you will falter; everyone does from time to time. But all is not lost! Just reach out to Jesus, and he will lift you up! And of course this is precisely what Matthew meant by the story. If it does not mean this, the story is no more important than some tabloid screed about a hillbilly getting probed aboard a UFO. And does it gain anything by being an accurate historical account (if

---

[11] Nau, *Peter in Matthew*, pp. 100–104.

you think it is)? Does it lose anything if you do not think it is? I do not see how. And, of course, leave it to Matthew to *double* the water-walkers! Looks like one is never enough!

Back for Seconds

Once again, let us assume for the sake of argument that Jesus did indeed miraculously multiply five loaves (barley dinner rolls, actually) and two fish as related in Mark 6:31, Matthew 14:13–21, Luke 9:10–17, and John 6:1–14 to feed a total of five thousand men. Did he go on to repeat the feat/feast with another *four* thousand, offering *seven* loaves and "a few small fish" as in Mark 8:1–10 and Matthew 15:32–39? Ah... *no*. Why not? The real miracle here would be the miraculous *stupidity of the disciples!* Both stories are much more likely to be variant versions of a single tale. "Oh yeah? Jesus was God, so he could have done it every day if he had wanted!" Presumably so, But the problem lies not with Jesus, but rather with the twelve. You can understand their puzzled skepticism the *first* time: "Is the boss crazy? How the hell are we going to feed *thousands* of hungry people with a few stale Kaiser rolls and a couple of cans of tuna?" Holy Mackerel—he does! But flash forward to a replay of the scene. It is *déjà vu* all over again! "Thousands of hungry mouths to feed, out in the middle of nowhere, nothing to give them? *Wait* a minute! Does this look familiar to any of you guys?" But nobody says that, do they? Instead, they show the same clueless astonishment they did the first time! Hel-*lo*! Later, Jesus reminds them of both incidents and asks if they learned anything from them. He rolls his eyes in exasperation: they have not. We really should have seen this moment immediately following the second time they protested. So what is going on here? We have better reason to be incredulous than they did!

Well, I will tell you: Mark was sorting through the various bits and pieces of Jesus tradition he wanted to assemble into a connected narrative. Some he found to be incompatible but included them anyway, like his juxtaposing of the two mutually exclusive answers to whether Elijah must appear before the Messiah arrives (Mark 9:4, 12–13). At least they're on the same subject! Kind of like *Nave's Topical Bible*. But sometimes, when a story/saying was merely redundant, he must have figured, "Why not include them both, maybe with some distracting filler in between so readers will not notice? If I omit either one, somebody is sure to squawk!"[12] Why do the numbers of audience members and of bread and fish vary between the two accounts? If you are retelling a story, perhaps a joke, secondary details are easy to forget and to replace, and numbers are the easiest of all! You see the same sort of thing when you compare the three versions of the Genesis adventure of the Patriarch who lies about his wife being his sister in hopes of saving his skin once the king sees what a knock-out she is and wants to add her to his harem. In Genesis 12:10–20, the couple is *Abram* and *Sarai*, who visit Egypt where they come to *Pharaoh's* attention. After a bit of narrative filler, the second version (Gen. 26:1–14, 16–17) changes the names, so the characters become *Abraham* and *Sarah*, and the foreign king is *Abimelech* of Gerar. More filler puts distance between that one and the third (Gen. chapter 20). This time the Israelite couple are *Isaac* and *Rebecca*, the king again being *Abimelech*. There is even another number problem because, to put sufficient space between the three versions, the compiler had to play fast and loose with the chronology, the result being that Sarai must be over ninety years old when she catches Pharaoh's lustful eye! *Hubba hubba!*

A kindred suggestion is that worked out by Paul J. Achtemeier,[13] who sniffed out Mark's seeming use of two parallel chains of miracle stories in Mark, both involving, first, a pair of sea miracles; second, a pair of exorcisms; third, a *pair of pairs* of healing miracles; fourth, a pair of miraculous feedings. The first version consists of Mark 4:35–41 (Stilling the Storm), 5:1–20 (Gerasene Demoniac), 5:21–43 (Woman with a Hemorrhage

---

[12] Think of how irate Bible fans greeted the 1946 publication of the Revised Standard Version with pious book-burning bonfires because the revisers had relegated to the footnotes some spurious passages, found only in late manuscripts, e.g. the Woman Taken in Adultery in John 7:53–8:11 and the Longer Ending of Mark, 16:9–20.

[13] Paul J. Achtemeier, *Jesus and the Miracle Tradition* (Eugene, OR: Cascade Books, 2008), "Toward the Isolation of Pre-Markan Miracle Catenae," pp. 55–86; "The Origin and Function of the Pre-Markan Catenae," pp. 87–116.

combined with Jairus' Daughter), and 6:34–44 (Feeding the 5,000). The second miracle-chain is made up of Mark 6:45–51 (Walking on Water), 7:24–31 (The Syro-Phoenician Woman), 7:32–37 (Healing the Deaf-Mute), 8:1–10 (Feeding the 4,000), and 8:22–26 (Healing the Blind Man). This serves to show how Mark inherited more than one version of several similar stories and had no scruples against using both.

Dennis R. MacDonald[14] offers a rather different explanation. Pursuing his hypothesis of Mark rewriting parts of the *Odyssey*, MacDonald proposes that Mark felt obliged to transpose a pair of outdoor crowd feedings with attendees seated in organized ranks and rows on the grass. Mark had two because Homer had two. Both hosts, Menelaus and Jesus, are magnanimous, going ahead with the feeding despite the doubts expressed by servants that there will be sufficient provisions. I do not find this suggestion compelling. But who knows? Maybe I am being as thick-headed as the disciples.

Major Minors

Many biblical contradictions go unnoticed because they are matters of easily-ignored details. But the details are more significant than you might think, and not just because it does hitherto-unsuspected serious damage to biblical authority. No, the news is good! We will see how a couple of these differences in detail add a new and edifying dimension to the texts in which they appear. Here I am indebted to acute observations by Günther Bornkamm, Gerhard Barth, and Joachim Held. Bornkamm[15] shows how Matthew uses Mark's Stilling of the Storm passage (Mark 4:35–41) to teach another lesson by calling attention to subtle editorial changes Matthew made in Mark. Mark 4:38 has the panicking disciples speak indignantly to Jesus, awakening him for help bailing out the capsizing boat: "Teacher, do you not care that we perish?" But in

---

[14] MacDonald, *Homeric Epics*, "Feasts for Thousands," pp. 83–90.

[15] Günther Bornkamm, "The Stilling of the Storm in Matthew." In Günther Bornkamm, Gerhard Barth, and Heinz Joachim Held, *Tradition and Interpretation in Matthew*. Trans. Percy Scott. New Testament Library (Philadelphia: Fortress Press, 1963), pp. 52–57.

Matthew 8:25 they are piously speaking in tones of Christian prayer: "Lord, save! We perish!" Mark 4:39 has Jesus stop the storm in its tracks, then ask rhetorically why the disciples were so upset. Did they not trust a providential Father? Jesus did; so he slept soundly.

But in Matthew 8:26 Jesus remarks on their paltry faith, *then* quiets the storm. Why reorder the narrative elements? He has repurposed the story as a lesson about *answered prayer*. Mark's focus is the divine power of Jesus, but Matthew can take that for granted. He shifts the focus to his readers to encourage them to pray boldly. You can call this a contradiction if you want, but then you are missing the point. The disciples did not say both "Don't you care? We are dying here!" *and* "Lord, save! We perish!" Jesus did not rebuke their lack of faith, still the storm, and then repeat his rebuke of their faithlessness verbatim again afterward! Such is the preposterous "solution" inerrantism offers to the "problem" it created.

In the mood for another sandwich? I hope so. Because Iron Chef Mark has combined two traditional healing stories, one about a woman with a menstrual flow that has continued unabated for, er, *twelve years*, the other of the resuscitation of a comatose girl twelve years old. Heinz Joachim Held[16] demonstrates that Matthew has made these interconnected stories, which were originally testimonials about the power of Jesus, into another encouragement to faithful prayer. In Mark 5:29 the old woman is healed as soon as she touches Jesus' prayer shawl. Jesus then congratulates her (5:34). Here Jesus is pictured as a dynamo of numinous energy. The old crone just plugs into it by touching his prayer shawl. Jesus is not even aware of her until he feels the discharge! But Matthew 9:22 reads differently: the healing comes *after* Jesus becomes telepathically aware of her faith and blesses her for it. In the same way, Matthew tells us, God answers the prayer of faith. But to get us to that, Matthew had to change the

---

[16] Heinz Joachim Held, "Matthew as Interpreter of the Miracle Stories." In Günther Bornkamm, Gerhard Barth, and Heinz Joachim Held, *Tradition and Interpretation in Matthew*. Trans. Percy Scott. (Philadelphia: Fortress Press, 1963) pp. 216, 240, 284–289.

order of events. And, yes, that creates a contradiction with Mark. But I for one think it is well worth it. If you want to fixate on snags in the weave, go ahead.

How about the bread slices? Mark split up an original story about Jairus' daughter and split it, inserting the story of the bleeding woman in the middle. There is something about the number twelve occurring in both (the duration of the menstruation and the age of the daughter) must have struck Mark as possessing some kabbalistic significance that escapes me. I am not sure how either story sheds light on the other. Apparently neither did Matthew. He restored what must have been the original unity of the Jairus story, and that created a minor conflict with Mark's version. Mark had Jairus consult Jesus while his daughter still lived and was sweating it out while some old bag kept waylaying Doctor Jesus. They were about to make the house call when one of Jairus' staff ran up with the bad news: the girl was now dead. As Jairus begins to freak out, Jesus tells him not to, since Jesus somehow knows the servant is mistaken: the maiden still lives. You know the rest. In the original, reconstructed by Matthew, Jairus' daughter would have been dead already when he came to Jesus for help (cf, John 11:21: "Lord, if you had been here, my brother would not have died."). It was clever of Mark to introduce the bleeding woman into the Jairus story in order to create narrative tension. The pressure on poor Jairus gets jacked up because the longer the old woman keeps chewing Jesus' ear, the shorter the time his daughter has to live!

6

Endgame and Execution

Gathered in Gethsemane

We enter an especially fascinating area of gospel comparison when we come near the denouement. Given its theological and devotional importance, it should surprise no one that momentous and pivotal developments will clash, be interpreted, and reinterpreted. We read of that might have happened and what "must" have happened. Prophecy transforms into narrative if not history, and it is never easy to tell the difference. The differences between stories themselves have stories to tell if we know how to listen. And by now I think perhaps we do.

Let us first join Jesus in the Garden of Gethsemane, where his prayers, which no one can have heard, are filled with desperation. Like any sane person, Jesus is greatly daunted by the prospect of imminent torment and death, one might even think, with no awareness that resurrection would reverse his doom, as if he did not know to expect it. We are well acquainted with the oddity that, despite repeated, explicit predictions of the Passion events, the twelve seem utterly flummoxed once things start breaking. Critical scholars rightly infer that these predictions are unhistorical "coming attractions" signals to the reader. They were never *heard* by Peter and the rest because never *spoken* to them. But might we not just as justifiably suspect that Jesus, too, was originally depicted as utterly unprepared and unaware of what was coming?

But all this pertains to inconsistencies within the Synoptic gospels. There is also a major contradiction between the Synoptics and John. And it is, once again, not some inexplicable goof or failure of historical memory. "Say, you remember when the rulers had that Jesus fellow put to death? Who was in charge? Was it not Herod? Herod *Antipas*? Herod *Agrippa*? Darned if *I* can keep them straight...." No, the discrepancies are the result of intentional editorial efforts. These writers were not stupid, but we are if we think so. And if we insist that the gospel authors were infallible oracles of God, no matter the abundant evidence to the contrary, we may be equally stupid.

Where were we? Ah! Gethsemane, right? Jesus was there with Matthew, Mark, and Luke eavesdropping. But not John! To be sure, he knew full well about those other accounts, but he could not concur. We cannot know what he knew or believed had happened there, but we *do* know what he says did *not* happen. For John, Jesus not only did not quail at the destiny marked out for him in blood. He could not have begged his Father to relieve him of the burden of impending execution. In fact, just the opposite! "Now is my soul troubled. And what shall I say? 'Father, save me from this hour'? No, for this purpose I have come to this hour. Father, glorify thy name." Then a voice came from heaven, "I have glorified it, and I will glorify it again" (John 12:27–28). This is clearly a scoffing repudiation of somebody else's version of events, not unlike Paul's in Galatians 1:20: "In what I am writing to you, before God, I do not lie!"

That Slippery Cross

How many times have you heard it told that Jesus embarked on the road to Calvary carrying his cross on his shoulder but then, because of his weakened condition after abuse, beating, and flogging, he collapsed under its splintery weight. And that then the Roman soldiers yanked a spectator out of the jeering crowd and ordered him to carry the cross the rest of the way. But if you are a close reader of the texts and do not drop them all into a theological blender, you will know that no one gospel says these things. Matthew, Mark and Luke say that Simon of Cyrene was drafted into service from step one, while John has Jesus carry his cross from beginning to end. Why? It is exactly the same reason John disdainfully dismissed any flinching by Jesus in the Garden: it seemed unbecoming for the Son of God! "What? You mean to tell me the guy who challenged hearers to take up their crosses to follow him *did not carry his own cross?* You gotta be *kidding* me!" Once you notice this, you might think twice before saying "I am not ashamed of the gospel of Christ." It is unfortunate.

On the Hot Seat

What did Jesus answer the high priest? Is there not another puzzling inconsistency between Jesus' supposed boldness and his seeming evasiveness when asked if he deems himself the Messiah? "You say that I am." Does that mean, "If you say so"? Apologists assure us that, no, this was an idiomatic way of saying, "You bet! Yessiree!" Pardon me, but I take that for wishful thinking. They want Jesus to boldly affirm their faith, so they pretend that he did. And so did an early copyist of Mark's gospel! As it happens, a few manuscripts attest what I believe to be the original reading at Mark 14:62: "You say [so]." This must have been what Matthew and Luke were reading in their (obviously) very early copies of Mark. If Mark had originally had Jesus say unequivocally "I am," why would his fellow Synoptists change it to "If you say so"? But I think the forthright answer ("I am") we now read is the result of a scribe who could not believe Jesus had returned so lame an answer ("You say") and altered it to what Jesus *should* have said and therefore *must* have said.

Jesus Who?

While Jesus was being interrogated inside, Peter was getting questioned out in the courtyard. Infamously, he wound up denying he knew Jesus or had ever even heard of him. To whom was Peter speaking when he denied Jesus? The four narratives do not quite agree. Inerrancy advocate Harold Lindsell[1] tried to iron out the differences by fitting the various denials into a sequence of *six* denials. Earlier apologists had judged that no less than *eight* would be required! Strauss[2] said they had underestimated the difficulties

---

[1] Harold Lindsell, *The Battle for the Bible* (Grand Rapids: Zondervan Publishing House, 1977).

[2] Strauss, *Life of Jesus*, p. 660.

and would really need *nine*! So how different *are* the addressees of the denials?

In Mark, Peter is quizzed first by "one of the maids of the high priest" (14:66), then second by the same maid again (verse 69), and third, by "the bystanders" (verse 70). Matthew has "a maid" (26:69), "another maid" (verse 71), and "the bystanders" (verse 73). It is pretty much the same as in Mark, but Matthew just half-remembered Mark's *maid's second question* as *a second maid's question*. No subtle shift of meaning. Luke 22:56 repeats the first maid, then "someone else" (verse 58), and finally "still another" (verse 59). So Luke also took Mark's second question as denoting a second questioner. For the third, he has, so to speak, narrowed down the group of "bystanders" to a single voice, quite possibly because he saw the silliness of having a crowd collectively speak the same words in unison! John has the maid posted at the door as Peter's first challenger. Second, John is happy enough to use the old gimmick, having the whole crowd, gathered around the fire like hobos in a train yard, speak as one as they take their turn questioning Peter (verse 25). In verse 26 Peter fends off "one of the servants of the high priest, a kinsman of the man whose ear Peter had cut off." This time we can see something of a progression, as Peter is getting deeper and deeper into trouble: first a maid, then a suspicious crowd, and finally someone who had a gripe against the Big Fisherman and could get him arrested. Yikes! But any way you cut it, you just cannot make the lists agree, any more than you can reconcile the genealogies of Joseph, er, I mean Jesus.

Is It Appointed to a Man to Die Once?

How did Judas Iscariot die? If you hate that creep so much that you think one death is not enough for him—it looks like you got your wish! Because you cannot reconcile the two New Testament accounts of his ending! Matthew has Judas recoil in self-loathing once he sees what he has brought upon Jesus and hang himself after returning the bounty money to the Sanhedrin. They judiciously decline to put the money back into the temple treasury, tainted as it is, so they launder it by using it to purchase a plot of ground where indigents can be interred. Now *that* is what you call righteous!

But over in Acts chapter one Luke supplies the obituary for Judas that he forgot to include in his gospel: the poor jerk spent the blood money himself to buy a plot of ground where he could, at his leisure, explode like Mr. Creosote in *Monty Python's The Meaning of Life*. Yes, you *could* translate the word as "fell headlong," but from *where*? Apologists spin out elaborate scenarios according to which Judas did not *himself* put the thirty silver coins into the hand of the real estate broker, but you could sort of *say* he bought the land since he gave the bucks to those who *did* actually buy it, so he "did" buy it, kind of. And maybe Judas was curious and went to see the land his pious paymasters had bought and then had a thought: "Hmmm… this would not be a bad place to string myself up!" And he did. But the Sanhedrin really did not give much of a damn about the old cemetery since they only bought it as a write-off anyway and did not even know Judas' corpse was hanging there rotting, eyes and nose plucked by vultures, carcass being used by vagrants for target practice—until the cheap rope snapped, causing him to fall the foot or two to the ground from a tree branch. But even though rigor mortis must have set in some time before, there had been such a multiplication of maggots inside him that they eventually split his belly open, scattering in a rain of squirming filth. Or something like that. Say, I guess that thing about Peter denying Jesus six or eight times does not sound so bad after all…

But, all harmonizing aside, the disgusting gushing of guts is more likely inspired derived from the yucky fate of Antiochus Epiphanes in 2 Maccabees 9:5–9.

> But the all-seeing Lord, the God of Israel, struck him an incurable and unseen blow. As soon as he ceased speaking he was seized with a pain in his bowels for which there was no relief and with sharp internal tortures—and that very justly, for he had tortured the bowels of others with many and strange inflictions….And so the ungodly man's body swarmed with worms, and while he was still living in anguish and pain, his flesh rotted away, and because of his stench the whole army felt revulsion at his decay.

7

The Art of Resurrection

Why Seek Ye the Historical
Among the Literary?

Apologists often admit that the gospel resurrection narratives seem to contradict one another. They go on to suggest possible ways in which all the details might be salvaged, combined in some great, synoptic mosaic. But these efforts strike me as no more plausible than Harold Lindsell's attempts to have Peter deny Jesus six times. Worse, they miss the point. The contradictions are not flies in the ointment; they are clues to a mystery. They do not so much spoil the evidence of the texts; instead, they are crucial evidence for understanding the texts. As Warfield might have said, they are indicia, pointers to the fictive character of the texts. Here is what I mean.

Mark 16, the earliest version of the Easter story, features the discovery of the empty tomb and the interpretive words of a young man, perhaps an angel. He announces that the absence of the body means that Jesus has risen. His words anticipate an appearance of Jesus, but none is offered. By itself, as Charles H. Talbert[1] has shown, the empty tomb story looks so much like other ancient "apotheosis" narratives, e.g., of Apollonius, Empedocles, Romulus, Hercules, etc., that it seems to me special pleading to insist that Mark's is however not one more of these legends but rather a report of historical fact.

Matthew and Luke, both using Mark as their basis, jump off the diving board provided by the abrupt ending of Mark, chapter 16,

---

[1] Charles H. Talbert, *What Is a Gospel? The Genre of the Canonical Gospels* (Philadelphia: Fortress Press, 1977); M. David Litwa, *Iesus Deus: The Early Christian Depiction of Jesus as a Mediterranean God* (Minneapolis: Fortress Press, 2014).

verse 8, but they jump in different directions. Especially since each evangelist's continuation bears ample marks of that writer's distinctive style and vocabulary, the most natural inference would be that each is making it up as he goes along. Similarly, various writers have tried their hand at finishing Dickens' fragment *The Mystery of Edwin Drood*. No one would take a second author's attempt to continue the abrupt ending of the first to be historical fact. The very nature of the enterprise shows the whole to be fiction. Matthew and Luke are, so to speak, each taking a crack at finishing *Edwin Drood*. They are writing fiction.

Matthew has altered Mark's unseemly ending so that the fleeing women obey the charge of the angel at the tomb. And he adds a sudden appearance of the Risen Jesus to the same women. But this Jesus merely repeats the charge the angel gave them, which implies that the Jesus episode is Matthew's doubling of Mark's young man episode. I think it likely that in this way Matthew sought to clear up the ambiguity left by Mark's description of the "young man"–who was he? An angel? Or Jesus himself? Matthew decided to cover both bases, so he divides the scene between an angel and Jesus, having them both bear essentially the same tidings.

The appearance on the Galilean hilltop is scarcely a story at all, but the barest narrative frame for a Matthean speech, betrayed by his distinctive vocabulary, "to disciple," "till the consummation of the age." Jesus, risen or not, can scarcely have given such a forthright Great Commission, or the uproar over Peter's visit to Cornelius is simply impossible to explain. We err in viewing this episode as history. It is not a report of what Jesus said to his disciples; surely it makes much better sense as a send-off by Matthew himself to those for whom he compiled the gospel, his missionaries to the Gentiles. It is they who know they must take this digest of teaching and relay it to the nations.

The business about the guards at the tomb is pure comedy: imagine them trying to get anyone to believe they knew the disciples stole the body when by their own account they were asleep at the time! Not even Sergeant Schultz on *Hogan's Heroes* would resort to such an excuse! And if Jesus had actually exited the tomb despite a cordon of armed soldiers, is it in any way possible to imagine that any other accounts of the events would have omitted it? Were Mark,

Luke, and John just economizing on ink? Was this "detail" unworthy of their notice? You just are asking not to be taken seriously if you say, "Oh, it happened all right; the other writers just did not happen to include it!" Let us rather account for the distinctiveness of Matthew's version by admitting that he embroidered and embellished his story, as he did also at the crucifixion account, where the death of Jesus prompts a mass resurrection of the saints who then appear in Jerusalem, all unnoticed by any other gospel.

What has Luke done, faced with Mark's seemingly washed-out bridge? He, too, has the women obey the angel–or rather the two men. Mark and Matthew had only one each. Again, let us not emulate the political spin-doctors by suggesting that there were actually two men or angels but that Matthew just did not happen to see one because the other was fatter and standing in front of him, or one was on a coffee break when Mark got there. Let us be honest with the text. There were not "actually" two, with Matthew and Mark "choosing" only one to mention. No, the truth is that Luke decided the story would read better if there were two heavenly spokesmen, just like the two men he has talking with Jesus at the Transfiguration and again with the Twelve at the ascension. Remember, the same author has the ascension itself occur on Easter Day in his gospel and forty days later in Acts. He simply cannot have been trying to report history in the first place. Luke was not an incompetent historian; he was a very competent creative writer!

Clues, Not Goofs

Why does Luke's speech of the two men at the tomb differ from that in Mark? Mark had the man say, "Go to Galilee; there you will see him, as he told you." Luke has changed this to "Remember how when he was in Galilee he told you the Son of Man must be delivered into the hands of men," etc. Luke wants salvation history to proceed from Jerusalem; thus his resurrection appearances happen in and around Jerusalem. He has simply lopped off the Galilean appearance Mark implied but neglected to narrate. He has the men at the tomb say what he knows no one actually said on that morning. It is not a question of deceit or error, "hoax or history."

This is a writer creatively rewriting a story. He has decided, for the sake of his story's flow, to exclude Galilean appearances, and it is to obscure Luke's theological agenda to pretend to harmonize him with Matthew by intercalating Matthew 28 in between Luke 24 and Acts 1. I am interested in what Matthew said, and in what Luke said. I am not interested in replacing them with some composite "Life of Christ in Stereo."

The wonderful story of the disciples on the Road to Emmaus, again, belongs to a certain legendary subgenre, that of the pious who "entertain angels unaware." One could point to Zeus and Hermes visiting Baucis and Philemon and various others, but the closest is a story, recorded four centuries before Luke, from the healing shrine of Asclepius at Epidaurus. A woman named Sostrata journeys to the holy site to be delivered of a dangerously long pregnancy. There she expects to have a dream of the savior who will tell her what to do. But nothing happens. Disappointed, she and her companions head for home again. Along the way they are joined by a mysterious stranger who asks the cause of their grief. Hearing her story, he bids them lay her stretcher down, and he cures her of what turns out to be a false pregnancy. Then he reveals his identity as Asclepius himself and is gone. It is not impossible that Luke borrowed the story, but that is not my point. The Emmaus story is recognizable as another tale of the same type. Why should we insist that the one is a legend but the other is historical?

The sudden appearance of the Risen Jesus among the dumbfounded disciples provides some of the favorite ammunition for apologists. We are told that the resurrection appearances must not have been subjective hallucinations since those who saw him had to be convinced despite their doubts. But this is to ignore the fact that such skepticism is a stock feature of miracle stories in general. The skepticism of the bystanders occurs again and again as a device to increase the suspense, to heighten the odds against which the wonder will seem all the greater. "How are we to feed all these people?" "Master, do you not care if we perish?" "'She is not dead but sleepeth,' and they laughed him to scorn." Asclepius restored the sight of a blind man who had an empty eye socket, despite the skeptical jeering of the crowd. Another man with a withered hand himself doubted the god could cure him, but he did, and Asclepius told him he must henceforth bear the nickname "Incredulous." The key is to see that the skepticism is simply a narrative device. The key to what? To understanding the text as what it is, not what it is not. It is literary, not historical.

As for John, he has put his own spin on the story of Jesus appearing amid the disciples in order to conform it to his private story of the spear-thrust. His Doubting Thomas story is cut from the same legendary cloth as its counterpart in Philostratus' *Life of Apollonius of Tyana*, while the miraculous catch of fish story (not even a resurrection story in Luke 5) seems to be borrowed from a Pythagoras story in which the exact number of the netted fish actually made some difference.

What does all this give us? My point is not to "debunk" the resurrection narratives as false witnesses, uncovering fatal inconsistencies between them. Like the false witnesses at the trial of Jesus: "their testimony did not agree." No, I have tried to show how the inconsistencies form a discernible pattern: that of various creative authors reworking a common draft to gain different effects. Not bad witnesses, but good story-tellers. Not on the witness stand, but around the campfire. And the parallels with other ancient stories indicate what genre the stories belong to: they are religious legends. Not a bad thing. Not unless you want them to be something else: historical reports. I don't want them to be one or the other. I just want to understand the texts, and I think I do.

Conclusion

Evangelical Old Testament scholar Gerald Sheppard once commented that "inerrancy" is not so much a coherent, descriptive concept as it is a shibboleth, a password into the Evangelical Christian community. If you do not parrot it like other churches chant the Nicene Creed, you are not welcome. Again, the magic word "inerrancy" is precisely analogous to the confession "I have a personal relation with Christ;" You have got to say it if you want to belong. Yet again, "inerrancy" functions like speaking in tongues in Pentecostalism: the token of having received the Baptism of the Holy Spirit. It is in this sense that biblical inerrancy is the foundation of Evangelical Christianity. We are assured by evangelical theologians that, if we give up belief in the infallibility of the Bible, the whole edifice will collapse to the ground. I think this is true, but not for the reasons its advocates aver. Here is what they say. If you cannot trust every statement any biblical author makes, even those which are admittedly insignificant in their own right, e.g. the exact dimensions of the Tabernacle, or the fact that the prophet Elisha was bald, you cannot trust the important ones either. But if the Bible is wrong about Michael and Satan arguing over who gets Moses' corpse, it might be just as wrong when it says Jesus rose from the dead. Why? Simply because the only reason to believe *anything* the Bible says is if it is contained in the Bible, the inspired Word of God. Apologists offer sham arguments for the Bible's accuracy, simply as a historical source. Even the most impressively erudite of these Public Relations men are transparently just shills for a party line.

In a fascinating book, *The Uses of Scripture in Recent Theology*, David H. Kelsey[2] maps out several very different ways in which the Bible functions as an authority for different types of churches and, as literary critic Stanley Fish[3] calls them, "interpretive communities." For some, it is the mythic symbols of the Bible that matters. For others, it is biblical materials as the substance of the all-important liturgy. Or as a book of exemplary character studies, etc. In the case of Evangelical Protestants, it is the authoritative doctrines and information based on "propositional revelation." How else could we know what is right and wrong? If there are many gods or one? Whether there is life after death? Whether Jesus rose from the dead? On such "fundamentals" Evangelicals brook no diversity of opinion. Express doubts on any one of these things in your church and see what happens. You will exile yourself from your faith community pretty fast.

Why, do you suppose, do all your church compatriots believe in *any*, much less *all*, of these doctrines? Is it sheer coincidence? I do not think so. They say they believe in the Trinity, but do you think there is the slightest chance they have reasoned out the question and settled on Trinitarianism rather than its theological

---

[2] David H. Kelsey, *The Uses of Scripture in Recent Theology* (Philadelphia: Fortress Press, 1975), "Doctrine and Concept," pp. 14–31.
[3] Stanley Fish, *Is There a Text in This Class? The Authority of Interpretive Communities* (Cambridge: Harvard University Press, 1982).

rivals Modalism or Tritheism? Why do they believe in the Trinity? If they were able to be honest with themselves, they would have to answer, "Because the people in my church are so nice!"

Or they might answer, as some of my students have, that they believe what their parents or their priest taught them, and they feel it would be disloyal to question it. In short, their beliefs are simply a function of their social existence. And this is no reason for believing anything.

The essentially non-rational character of "belief in the Bible" is made even clearer when you examine the strategies of harmonizing biblical contradictions. It is not so much the issues upon which contradictory texts disagree. Again, the issue, the danger, is that the necessity to choose one contradictory verse over another would destroy the very basis for believing *either* verse, or *any* verse, since the mere presence of a verse in the Bible is the only guarantee it is to be believed. If we decide James is right and Paul is wrong (or vice versa), there will no longer be sufficient reason to believe in either one! And remember, we are talking about *beliefs*, not opinions, empirically unverifiable claims, not reasoned conclusions. The believer is afraid of the latter, because our reasoning is not infallible, but the Bible (supposedly) *is*. And we cannot afford to be mistaken, at least on the big-ticket items, because Jehovah will not forgive that "sin."

When a biblicist finds himself cornered by what he has learned to call an "apparent" contradiction, what does he do? He deceives himself. He reinterprets the verse he does not like, that would undermine his theology, as if it agreed with the passage he *does* like, as when a Calvinist who believes in the Limited Atonement doctrine (Jesus died only for the predestined elect) tries to convince himself that in John 3:16 ("For God so loved the world that he gave his only-begotten Son, that whosoever believeth in him should not perish but should have eternal life") "the world" *means* "the elect." It might sound implausible to you, but the Calvinist finds it quite plausible, even probable, since his criterion for plausibility is "Does it fit my theology?" In fact, however, the harmonizer is doing the very thing he thinks he repudiates: he *is* silencing one biblical statement to allow its opposite number to speak. He *is* choosing what in the Bible to believe and what in the Bible *not* to believe. Only he cannot bear to realize it. This selectivity means that, while the fundamentalist imagines he is saying, "Speak, Lord, for thy servant heareth" (1 Sam. 3:10) he is actually saying to the Bible, "Be muzzled!" (Mark 1:25).

Do you not think it is time to "put away childish things"? And I do not mean the Bible. That is not one of the childish things. But there is a childish way of *reading* it, and many, many people, who are otherwise erudite and emotionally mature, have never abandoned the Toyland of credulous fundamentalism. To do it, of course, one would have to sacrifice certain childish delights, including some facile certainties. But I am sure you will come out ahead. The Bible will be no less loveable, no less fascinating. I guarantee you would find unsuspected depths and dimensions in it. And its wisdom will not stop being wise. Personally, I believe there is nothing more pious than understanding the text.

Bibliography

Achtemeier, Paul J. "Toward the Isolation of Pre-Markan Miracle Catenae," In *Jesus and the Miracle Tradition*, 55–86. Eugene, OR: Cascade Books, 2008.

———. "The Origin and Function of the Pre-Markan Catenae," In *Jesus and the Miracle Tradition*, 87–116. Eugene, OR: Cascade Books, 2008.

Atwilll, Joseph. *Caesar's Messiah: The Roman Conspiracy to Invent Jesus*. Charleston, SC: CreateSpace, 2011.

Bornkamm, Günther, "The Stilling of the Storm in Matthew." Translated by Percy Scott. In *Tradition and Interpretation in Matthew*, 52–57. Philadelphia: Fortress Press, 1963.

Brown, Raymond E. *The Birth of the Messiah: A Commentary on the Infancy Narratives in Matthew and Luke*. Garden City: Doubleday, 1977.

———. *The Community of the Beloved Disciple: The Life, Loves, and Hates of an Individual Church in New Testament Times*. New York: Paulist Press, 1979.

Bultmann, Rudolf. "Is Exegesis without Presuppositions Possible?" Translated and edited by Schubert M. Ogden. In *Existence and Faith: Shorter Writings of Rudolf Bultmann*, 289–296. Living Age Books/Meridian Books/World Publishing, 1960.

———. *The Gospel of John: A Commentary*. Translated by G.R. Beasley-Murray, R.W.N. Hoare, and J.K. Riches. Philadelphia: Westminster Press, 1971.

———. *The History of the Synoptic Tradition*. Translated by John Marsh. New York: Harper & Row, 1968.

———. *Theology of the New Testament*. Translated by Kendrick Groebel. New York: Scribners, 1951.

———. *Jesus Christ and Mythology*. New York: Scribners, 1958.

Barker, Margaret. "The Evidence of the New Testament." In *The Great Angel: A Study of Israel's Second God*, 213–232. Louisville: Westminster/John Knox Press, 1992.

Boyarin, Daniel. *The Jewish Gospels: The Story of the Jewish Christ*. New York: The New Press, 2012.

Casey, Maurice. "The Son of Man Problem." In *Son of Man: The Interpretation and Influence of Daniel 7*, 224–240. London: S.P.C.K., 1979.

Chapman, Graham, et al. *Monty Python's Life of Brian (of Nazareth)*. New York: Ace Books, 1979.

Chilton, Bruce. "The *Talmid* of John." In *Rabbi Jesus: An Intimate Biography*, 41–63. New York: Doubleday Image. 2000.

Cohen, Daniel. *The New Believers: Young Religion in America*. New York: Ballantine Books, 1975.

Conzelmann, Hans. *The Theology of St. Luke*. Translated by Geoffrey Buswell. New York: Harper & Row, 1960.

Cope, Lamar O. "The Good Is One– Mt 19:16–22 and Prov 3:35–4:4," In *Matthew: A Scribe Trained for the Kingdom of Heaven*, 111–120. Catholic Biblical Quarterly Washington D.C.: Catholic Biblical Association, 1976.

Dahl, Nils Alstrup. *The Crucified Messiah and other Essays*. Minneapolis: Augsburg Publishing House, 1974.

Dibelius, Martin. *The Message of Jesus Christ: The Tradition of the Earliest Christian Communities*. Translated by Frederick C. Grant. New York: Scribners, 1939.

Downing, F. Gerald. *Cynics and Christian Origins*. Edinburgh: T&T Clark, 1992.

Ehrman, Bart D. *The Orthodox Corruption of Scripture: The Effect of Early Christological Controversies on the Text of the New Testament*. New York: Oxford University Press, 2011.

Festinger, Leon, Henry W. Riecken, and Stanley Schachter, *When Prophecy Fails: A Social and Psychological Study of a Modern Group that Predicted the Destruction of the World*. New York: Harper & Row, 1964.

Franklin, Eric. *Christ the Lord: A Study in the Purpose and Theology of Luke-Acts*. Philadelphia: Westminster Press, 1975.

Fish, Stanley. *Is There a Text in This Class? The Authority of Interpretive Communities*. Cambridge: Harvard University Press, 1982.

Fowler, Robert M. *Let the Reader Understand: Reader-Response Criticism and the Gospel of Mark*. Minneapolis: Fortress Press, 1991.

Fuller, Reginald H. *Interpreting the Miracles*. London: SCM Press, 1963.

Halley, Henry H. *Halley's Bible Handbook: An Abbreviated Bible Commentary*. Grand Rapids: Zondervan Publishing House, 1965.

Harnack, Adolf. *What Is Christianity?* Translated by Thomas Bailey Saunders. New York: Harper & Row, 1957.

Harrison, Everett F. "Criteria of Biblical Errancy." In *Christianity Today,* edited by Frank E. Gaebelein. 86–90. New York: Pyramid Books, 1968.

Held, Heinz Joachim. "Matthew as Interpreter of the Miracle Stories." Translated by Percy Scott. In *Tradition and Interpretation in Matthew*, 216, 240, 284–289. Philadelphia: Fortress Press, 1963.

Jeremias, Joachim. *The Parables of Jesus*. Translated by S.H. Hooke. New York: Scribners, 1972.

———. *Theology of the New Testament*. Translated by John Bowden. London: SCM Press, 1971.

———. *Jesus' Promise to the Nations*. Translated by S.H. Hooke. London: SCM Press, 1967.

Jones, Terry and Terry Gilliam. dir. *Monty Python's The Meaning of Life*. 1983. England, UK: Universal Pictures, DVD.

Käsemann, Ernst. "Paul and Early Catholicism." Translated by Wilfred F. Bunge. In *New Testament Questions of Today*, 236–251. Philadelphia: Fortress Press, 1969.

Kelsey, David H. "Doctrine and Concept." In *The Uses of Scripture in Recent Theology*, 14–31. Philadelphia: Fortress Press, 1975.

Knox, John. *Chapters in a Life of Paul*. New York: Abingdon Press, 1950.

Klausner, Joseph. *Jesus of Nazareth: His Life, Times, and Teaching*. Translated by Herbert Danby. New York: Menorah Publishing, 1979.

Kugel, James L. *The Idea of Biblical Poetry: Parallelism and Its History*. Baltimore: Johns Hopkins Press, 1992.

Kuhn, Thomas S. "Anomaly and the Emergence of Scientific Discoveries." In *The Structure of Scientific Revolutions*, 52–61. Chicago: University of Chicago Press, 1962.

Kümmel, Werner Georg. *Promise and Fulfilment: The Eschatology of Jesus*. Translated by Dorothea M. Barton. London: SCM Press, 1961.

Ladd, George Eldon. *The Presence of the Future: The Eschatology of Biblical Realism*. Grand Rapids: Eerdmans, 1974.

Lindsell, Harold. *The Battle for the Bible*. Grand Rapids: Zondervan Publishing House, 1977.

Litwa, M. David. *Iesus Deus: The Early Christian Depiction of Jesus as a Mediterranean God*. Minneapolis: Fortress Press, 2014.

Loisy, Alfred. *The Gospel and the Church*. Translated by Christopher Home. Philadelphia: Fortress Press, 1976.

Longenecker, Richard. "Jewish Hermeneutics in the First Century." In *Biblical Exegesis in the Apostolic Period*, 19–50. Grand Rapids: Eerdmans, 1975.

MacDonald, Dennis R. "Speluncular Savages." In *The Homeric Epics and the Gospel of Mark*, 63–76. New Haven: Yale University Press, 2000.

———. "Feasts for Thousands." In *The Homeric Epics and the Gospel of Mark*, 83–90. New Haven: Yale University Press, 2000.

Meagher, John C. *Clumsy Construction in Mark's Gospel: A Critique of Form- and Redaktionsgeschichte*. New York and Toronto: Edwin Mellon Press, 1979.

Mowinckel, Sigmund. *He That Cometh: The Messiah Concept in the Old Testament and Later Judaism*. New York: Abingdon Press, 1954.

Nau, Arlo J. *Peter in Matthew: Discipleship, Diplomacy, and Dispraise*. Collegeville, MN: Liturgical Press, 1992.

Neusner, Jacob. *A Life of Rabban Yohanan ben Zakkai Ca. 1–80 C.E.* 6, (1962): 60–61.

Nesfield-Cookson, Bernard. *The Mystery of the Two Jesus Children and the Descent of the Spirit of the Sun*. Forest Run: Temple Lodge Publishing, 2005.

Price, Robert M. "Antioch's Aftershocks: Rereading Galatians and Matthew after Saldarini." *When Judaism and Christianity Began: Essays in Memory of Anthony J. Saldarini. Volume One: Christianity in the Beginning* 85, (2004): 231–250.

———. "The Synoptic Apocalypse and the Son of Man" in *Journal of Higher Criticism* Vol. 15, no. 1, 4–22.

Rogers, Roswell and Ed James, writers. *Father Knows Best*. Season 4, episode 11, "Mr. Beal Meets his Match." Directed by Peter Tewksbury, featuring James Anderson Sr., Jane Wyatt, Elinor Donahue, Billy Gray, Lauren Chapin and John Williams. Aired December 11th 1957 in broadcast syndication.

Salm, Rene. *The Myth of Nazareth: The Invented Town of Jesus.* Cranford: American Atheist Press, 2008.

Schaberg, Jane. "Matthew's Account of Jesus' Origin." In *The Illegitimacy of Jesus: A Feminist Theological Interpretation of the Infancy Narratives,* 20–77. San Francisco: Harper & Row, 1987.

Sigal, Phillip. *The Halakhah of Jesus of Nazareth According to the Gospel of Matthew.* Society of Biblical Literature Studies in Biblical Literature, no. 18 (2007): 87.

Schechter, Solomon. *Some Aspects of Rabbinic Theology.* New York: Macmillan, 1910.

Scheler, Max. *Problems of a Sociology of Knowledge.* Translated by Manfred S. Frings. London: Routledge & Kegan Paul, 1980.

Schmithals, Walter. *The Office of Apostle in the Early Church.* Translated by John E. Steely. Nashville: Abingdon Press, 1969.

Scholem, Gershom. *Sabbatai Sevi the Mystical Messiah.* Translated by R.J. Zwi Werblowsky. Princeton: Princeton University Press, 1973.

Schonfield, Hugh J. "North Palestinian Sectarians and Christian Origins," In *The Passover Plot: New Light on the History of Jesus,* 199–206. New York: Bantam Books, 1967.

———. *The Authentic New Testament.* New American Library/A Mentor Book, 1958.

Schottroff, Louise. "Tax Collectors." Translated by Matthew J. O'Connell. In *Jesus of Nazareth the Hope of the Poor,* 7–13. Maryknoll: Orbis Books, 1986.

Schmidt, Karl Ludwig. *The Place of the Gospels in the General History of Literature*. Translated by Byron R. McCane. Columbia: University of South Carolina, 2002.

Schmiedel, Paul Wilhelm. "Gospels." In *Encyclopaedia: A Critical Dictionary of the Literary, Political and History, the Archæology, Geography and Natural History of the Bible*. T.K.Cheyne and J. Sutherland Black, eds. London: Adam and Charles Black, 1914.

Schweitzer, Albert. *The Mystery of the Kingdom of God: The Secret of Jesus' Messiahship and Passion*. Translated by Walter Lowrie. New York: Schocken Books, 1964.

————. *The Quest of the Historical Jesus: A Critical Study of Its Progress from Reimarus to Wrede*. Translated by W. Montgomery 1906; rpt. New York: Macmillan, 1968.

Shepherd, A.P. *Scientist of the Invisible: Rudolf Steiner*. Vermont: Inner Traditions International, 1983.

Smith, Morton. *Jesus the* Magician. San Francisco: Harper & Row, 1978.

Steiner, Rudolf. "The Two Jesus Children." Translated by D.S. Osmond with Owen Barfield. Printed lecture from series presented at Basle, Switzerland, September 15th–26th 1909.

Stendahl, Krister. *The School of St. Matthew and its Use of the Old Testament*. Philadelphia: Fortress Press, 1969.

Strauss, David Friedrich. *The Life of Jesus Critically Examined*. Translated by George Eliot (Mary Ann Evans). Philadelphia: Fortress Press, 1972.

Suggs, M. Jack. *Wisdom, Christology, and Law in Matthew's Gospel*. Cambridge: Harvard University Press, 1970.

Talbert, Charles H. *What Is a Gospel? The Genre of the Canonical Gospels*. Philadelphia: Fortress Press, 1977.

Trobisch, David. *The First Edition of the New Testament*. New York: Oxford University Press, 2000.

————. "Who Published the New Testament?" *Free Inquiry*, 28 no. 1 (2007–2008): 30–33.

Theissen, Gerd. "The Wandering Radicals: Light Shed by the Sociology of Literature on the Early Transmission of Jesus Sayings." Translated by Margaret Kohl. In *Social Reality and the Early Christians: Theology, Ethics, and the New Testament*, 33–59. Minneapolis: Fortress Press, 1992.

Thiering, Barbara. "The Pesher Technique." In *Jesus the Man: A New Interpretation from the Dead Sea Scrolls*, 28–35. Transworld Publisher/A Corgi Book, 1993.

Weeden, Theodore J. *Mark: Traditions in Conflict*. Philadelphia: Fortress Press, 1971.

Werner, Martin. *The Formation of Christian Dogma*. Translated by S.G.F. Brandon. Boston: Beacon Press, 1965.

Wheless, Joseph A. *Is It God's Word? An Exposition of the Fables and Mythology of the Bible and of the Impostures of Theology*. New York: Alfred A. Knopf, 1926.

Wrede, William. *The Messianic Secret*. Translated by J.C.G. Greig. Edinburgh: James Clarke, 1905.

Vermes, Geza. *Jesus the Jew: A Historian's Reading of the Gospels*. London: Fontana/Collins, 1976.

Valliant, James S. and Warren Fahy. *Creating Christ: How Roman Emperors Invented Christianity*. Hertford, NC: Crossroad Press, 2018.